Martha Baum
Pamela Twiss
Editors

Social Work Intervention in an Economic Crisis: The River Communities Project

Pre-publication
REVIEWS,
COMMENTARIES,
EVALUATIONS . . .

"**T**his book makes a powerful statement regarding the impact of the dramatic decline of the steel industry on numerous mill towns in western Pennsylvania. It documents the disastrous impact on individuals and families, and on the communities themselves. However, it also serves as a testament to the strength, resiliency, and commitment of many of the residents of these communities in transition.

This publication is notable in providing several excellent examples of community-based social research. The various studies include an emphasis on a range of individuals being affected by this

economic tragedy: families, women, youth, and the elderly. The specifics regarding data collection methodologies and tools can be extremely helpful to any student of social research.

Perhaps the best part of this book is the story it tells about 'action'–the ideas, initiatives, and programs that emerged from the research, and from the partnerships involving the university, community organizations, and the residents themselves. By providing rapid feedback to the communities, and by providing assistance in the planning and community development process, the School of Social Work clearly provided needed resources to these communities. Ultimately, the educational process was shifted into the community, with students working on a variety of community organizing, educational, and economic development strategies.

This publication sets a standard for universities in terms of the types of meaningful roles they can play in supporting and sustaining communities. These examples of university-community partnerships should be required reading for university administrators."

Kenneth J. Jaros, PhD
Director, Public Health
Social Work Training Program,
University of Pittsburgh

"**S**ocial Work Intervention in an Economic Crisis: The River Communities Project reviews the impact of the massive disruption created in the Pittsburgh region by the collapse of the heavy metal industry and the role of the University of Pittsburgh School of Social Work in cooperation with affected communities in documenting the human tragedy involved in economic decline and of their struggle to revitalize the region.

The research provides pertinent, unique, and important data on how economic decline alters the very marrow of community–destabilizing individuals, families, and public and private institutions, creating in its wake heightened family, ethnic, and racial tension, and developing in some a sense of skepticism and hostility to the institutions that were the foundation of their lives before the economic collapse. Out of the shock and trauma, there developed a movement to recreate the industrial valleys into a new economy. The story of the resilience, energy, and organizational ability of ordinary citizens is an antidote to the despair and frustration that grips the nation today.

The book also documents how an academic institution with committed leadership can use its resources, especially faculty and students, to work cooperatively with communities to help them understand and respond to economic changes.

Finally, the work documents the powerful learning experience action research is for both faculty and students."

Morton Coleman, PhD
Professor, School of Social Work,
University of Pittsburgh

"This book is a fascinating and detailed account of a unique partnership between a major School of Social Work and an economically devastated region. This case study provides an excellent account of the way in which a School of Social Work is able to reach out and work with communities in helping to analyze and provide solutions in times of economic and social distress over a ten-year period. The authors provide an enriching account of the many forms of intervention and research efforts engaged in this combined effort. It is one of the very few books from the field of social work that documents social work's involvement in macro practice.

In these times The River Communities Project has much to offer that would enrich our curriculum content. It describes a process of working with the community; it is a study of problem identification and problem-solving processes, a study of social and economic forces that affect the lives of people; it describes the involvement of social work faculty and students as they work in the community; and it has implications for social work intervention. I would recommend this book highly as a resource for social work because so little has been written about macro practice and the university-community partnership in the field of social work in the past twenty years."

Marvin D. Feit, PhD
Professor, Director,
University of Akron
School of Social Work

The Haworth Press, Inc.

Social Work Intervention in an Economic Crisis
The River Communities Project

HAWORTH Social Work Practice
Carlton E. Munson, DSW, Senior Editor

New, Recent, and Forthcoming Titles:

Social Work Intervention in an Economic Crisis
The River Communities Project

Martha Baum
Pamela Twiss
Editors

The Haworth Press
New York • London

The Haworth Press, Inc., 10 Alice Street, Binghamton, NY 13904-1580

Cover designed by Monica L. Seifert.

Library of Congress Cataloging-in-Publication Data

Social work intervention in an economic crisis: the River Communities Project/Martha Baum, Pamela Twiss, editors.
    p. cm.
    Includes bibliographical references (p.   ) and index.
    ISBN 0-7890-6036-1 (alk. paper)
    1. University of Pittsburgh. Graduate School of Social Work. River Communities Project. 2. Community development–Pennsylvania–Pittsburgh Region–Case studies. 3. Social work with the unemployed–Pennsylvania–Pittsburgh Region–Case studies. 4. Deindustrialization–Pennsylvania–Pittsburgh Region. 5. Plant shutdowns–Pennsylvania–Pittsburgh Region. I. Baum, Martha. II. Twiss, Pamela
HN80.P6S64 1996
307.1′4′0974886–dc20   96-357
                                                             CIP

To Professor James Cunningham, whose boundless energy, commitment, and belief in the potential of people and their communities made the River Communities Project possible.

CONTENTS

ABOUT THE EDITORS

Martha Baum, PhD, is Professor of Social Work at the University of Pittsburgh in Pennsylvania, where she has been on the faculty since 1973. Co-author of *The Aging: A Guide to Public Policy* and *Growing Old: A Societal Perspective*, Dr. Baum has also written numerous articles that have appeared in journals such as *The Gerontologist*, the *Journal of Health and Social Policy*, and the *Journal of Education for Social Work*. Her research interests include social support networks for the elderly, caregiving and multigenerational families, and the roles of women in families.

Pamela Twiss, PhD, is Assistant Professor of Social Work at Marywood College in Scranton, Pennsylvania. Her previous work experience includes positions as Research Consultant for the Great Lakes Behavioral Research Institute in Pittsburgh and as Project Coordinator for the River Communities Project at the University of Pittsburgh's School of Social Work. Her research interests include poverty and associated problems, unemployment, formal and informal networks in small communities and their strengths and weaknesses in meeting human needs, and experimental education.

ABOUT THE AUTHORS

Phyllis D. Coontz, PhD, Associate Professor, Graduate School of Public and International Affairs, University of Pittsburgh, Pennsylvania

Kathy Fleissner, PhD, MPH, Assistant Professor of Social Work, Clarion University of Pennsylvania

Lambert Maguire, PhD, Professor and Chairman of Direct Practice, School of Social Work, University of Pittsburgh, Pennsyvlania

Judith A. Martin, PhD, Professor, School of Social Work, University of Pittsburgh, Pennsylvania

Mary Lou O'Kennedy, MSW, Manager of the County Wexford Partnership, County Wexford, Ireland

Mary H. Page, MSW, LSW, PhD, Professor Emeritus, School of Social Work, University of Pittsburgh, Pennsylvania

Robin K. Rogers, MA, MSSW, Executive Director of the Commission for Workforce Excellence in Pittsburgh, Pennsylvania

Barbara K. Shore, ACSW, PhD, MPH, Distinguished Service Professor Emerita, School of Social Work, University of Pittsburgh, Pennsylvania

Myrna Silverman, PhD, Associate Professor of Health Services Administration and Anthropology, University of Pittsburgh, Pennsylvania

Edward W. Sites, PhD, Professor, School of Social Work, University of Pittsburgh, Pennsylvania

Hide Yamatani, PhD, Professor, School of Social Work, University of Pittsburgh, Pennsylvania; President of Excellence Research Inc., Pittsburgh, Pennsylvania

Contributors

The following list of contributors is an effort to acknowledge the many people who played a part in the River Communities Project through its research and demonstration phases. It must be noted that this list is certainly incomplete. There are undoubtedly people who have been neglected who should have been listed, and for that, the editors apologize in advance. Of special note, this list covers only the River Communities Project and does not acknowledge the great efforts made by those who participated in more recent developments stemming from the River Communities Project–for example, the Poverty, Race, and Opportunities studies, an ongoing project of the University of Pittsburgh's School of Social Work.

Executive Committee of the River Communities Project
University of Pittsburgh, School of Social Work

David E. Epperson, Dean, School of Social Work,
and Director of the Project

Tony Tripodi, Associate Dean, School of Social Work

Jim Cunningham, Principal Investigator

David Biegel, School of Social Work, Co-Investigator

Morton Coleman, School of Social Work, Co-Investigator

George McClomb, School of Social Work, Co-Investigator

Mary H. Page, School of Social Work, Co-Investigator

Hide Yamatani, School of Social Work, Co-Investigator

Vijai Singh, Director, University of Pittsburgh's University Center
for Social and Urban Research

Carolyn Louderback, Budgets and Finance

Pamela Martz, Coordinator

Robin K. Rogers, Research Associate

FACULTY	POSITION/SCHOOL/DEPARTMENT
Roger Ahlbrandt	Associate Dean, Graduate School of Business
Martha Baum	Professor, Social Work
Phyllis D. Coontz	Professor, Graduate School of Public and International Affairs
Anne Jones	Professor, Social Work
Lambert Maguire	Professor, Social Work
Aaron Mann	Associate Professor, Social Work
Michael Margolis	Professor, Political Science
Judith A. Martin	Professor, Social Work
Barbara K. Shore	Professor, Social Work
Myrna Silverman	Professor, Graduate School of Public Health
Edward W. Sites	Professor, Social Work
Kiernan Stenson	Professor, Social Work

All faculty listed were, at the time of the project, faculty at the University of Pittsburgh.

STUDENTS INVOLVED IN RCP RESEARCH

Students	School Degree Program	School/ Department
Michael Barfield	MSW	Social Work
Elizabeth Blocher	MSW	Social Work
Sr. Carol Burger	MSW	Social Work
Robert E. Burtt	MA	Political Science
Cathy Cairns	MSW	Social Work

Students	School Degree Program	School/ Department
Denys Candy	MSW	Social Work
Margaret Chorpenning	MSW	Social Work
Pauline Cooper	MSW	Social Work
Rita P. Costa	MSW	Social Work
Mike Eichler	MSW	Social Work
Kathy Fleissner	PhD	Social Work
Shannon Guy	MSW	Social Work
Matthew Hawkins	MSW	Social Work
Anita Hrebinko	MSW	Social Work
Judy Ismail-Beigi	MSW	Social Work
Peter Kelley	MSW	Social Work
Barbara Kunschner	MSW	Social Work
Robina Linear	MSW	Social Work
Richard L. Losasso	MSW	Social Work
Christa McClusky	MSW	Social Work
Jeffrey McLaughlin	MPA	Graduate School of Public and International Affairs
Willie E. McLendon	MSW	Social Work
Sheila McVey	MSW	Social Work
Susanne K. Miller	MSW	Social Work
Charles H. Monsour	MSW	Social Work
Stacy Moore	MSW	Social Work
Jeff Morris	MSW	Social Work
Mary Ohmer	MSW	Social Work
Mary Lou O'Kennedy	MSW	Social Work
William Page	MSW	Social Work
Teresa Parton-Lopez	MPH	Graduate School of Public Health
Carl Redwood, Jr.	MSW	Social Work
Celestine Robb	MSW	Social Work
Robin K. Rogers	PhD	Social Work
Barbara Sahlaney	MSW	Social Work
Chaiw-Yi Shih	MSW	Social Work
Betty Simonds	MPH	Graduate School of Public Health

Students	School Degree Program	School/ Department
Carla Smith	MSW	Social Work
Kay Snyder	MSW	Social Work
Audrey Spencer	PhD	Social Work
Cheryl Trotter	MSW	Social Work
Pamela (Martz) Twiss	PhD	Social Work
Leanne Unites	MSW	Social Work
Willie A. Wise, Jr.	MSW	Social Work
Joe Witherspoon	MSW	Social Work
James K. Yost	MSW	Social Work

Foundations and Organizations Providing Financial Support to RCP Projects

Appalachian Regional Commission
Beaver-Butler Presbytery
Beaver Community Services Block Grant
Buhl Foundation
Catholic Diocese of Pittsburgh
Community Donations
Federated Investors, Inc.
H. J. Heinz Endowment
Legislature, Commonwealth of Pennsylvania
Martin M. Dudas Foundation
Mellon Bank Foundation
Mid-Mon Valley Economic Revitalization Program
National Center for Neighborhood Enterprise
People's Natural Gas Company
PPG Industries Foundation
Staunton Farm Foundation
The Pittsburgh Foundation
Vira Heinz Endowment

Individual Contributors from the Community

AAUD (Aliquippa Alliance for Unity and Development),
  D E' Andre Abercrombie

Aliquippa Ministerial Association
  Sr. Carol Burger

AAUD
  Cathy Cairns

AAUD
  Elaine Carr

AAUD
  Pauline Cooper

ELDI (East Liberty Development, Inc.)
  Louise Craighead

State Senator, Homestead
  Michael Dawida

Mon Valley Initiative
  Jo DeBolt

United Way
  Gerald Dill

Dentist, Monessen
  Martin Dudas

Professor, Pennsylvania State University, Beaver Campus
  Sidney Elkin

Community of Celebration, Aliquippa
  Bill Farra

ELDI
  David Feehan

Teacher, Monessen High School
  Vicki Furnier

AAUD
  Diane Gilbert

NAACP (National Association for the Advancement
of Colored People)
Leon Haley

AAUD
Leo Katroppa

ELDI
Mary Kellers

ELDI
Karen LaFrance

Center for Social and Urban Research, University of Pittsburgh
Steven Manners

Program Officer, Heinz Endowments
Patricia McElligott

AAUD
Jennifer Henderson Milliner

Aliquippa Hospital
Diane Modany

Monessen
Tom and Amy Rapp

Allegheny County Commission on Workforce Excellence
Robin Rogers

University of Pittsburgh
Alta Rusman

McKeesport Hospital
Marlene Schick

Executive Director, Human Services Center Corporation
Tracy Soska

Principal, Monessen High School
Fred Usher

Youth Enterprise Steering Committee, Monessen
Rita Whatule

Superintendent, School District of the City of Monessen
Tom Wilkinson

NAACP in Aliquippa
Lorenzo Williams

Foreword

During the deep economic recession of the 1980s, no region in the nation was hit harder than that around Pittsburgh. Blessed with rivers, forests, and rich natural gas and coal resources, this region of 2.65 million people reigned for years as one of the world's leading producers of basic steel. In the past decade it has been decimated by plant closings and the loss of 40 percent of its well-paying industrial jobs. Some mill towns have had to go into bankruptcy, and thousands of young people have left the area for more promising opportunities elsewhere.

Many institutions in this southwestern corner of Pennsylvania responded early to the crisis with efforts to foster survival and rebuilding. The University of Pittsburgh, especially through its School of Social Work, was one of the large institutions that became involved. The School, utilizing its ongoing engagement with the region's networks of social agencies, implemented a coordinated response called the River Communities Project so that policy research, demonstration programs, and expanded community service could be undertaken. The project has focused on understanding the human impact of the crisis, and allowed the School to play a role in the recovery efforts of families and small industrial communities. This book is part of a continuing effort to deepen understanding of the tragedy and enhance recovery.

For most of its history, the School of Social Work has had a close working relationship with the people of the region. In the 1950s, Professor Meyer Schwartz began to arrange social work graduate student field placements with activist neighborhood groups. This pioneering work led to the nation's first two-year master's degree program in community organization. Faculty of the School helped to plan and carry out Pittsburgh's neighborhood-oriented antipoverty program during the 1960s.

Through the 1970s a series of studies that focused on resident attachment and on the effectiveness of differential strategies used by neighborhood organizations was conducted in city neighborhoods. Out of this work came the Pittsburgh Neighborhood Atlas (a compendium of services and facilities), as well as a series of articles and books. From the 1950s through the 1970s, the School offered advocacy, planning, and development services to community nonprofit organizations. By the 1980s the School of Social Work was well prepared to study the profound tragedy that came with the collapse of the steel industry.

During the 1980s Pittsburgh underwent a social and economic transition that overwhelmed many of the small smokestack communities stretched along the region's large river system. Their struggles became an area of concentration for the School. This volume synthesizes much of that work. The chapters that follow describe the devastation inflicted on individuals, households, and whole communities, the responses of local institutions, and the roles of informal and formal support networks. Finally, they offer proposals for new societal mechanisms that might reduce the impact of future recessions.

Findings have already been used by policymakers in government and in the nonprofit sector. In some of the communities under study, the School has moved beyond research and policy recommendations and has assisted residents and institutional leaders in launching programs for unity, job creation, and planned development.

We hope that by publishing these findings and proposals in one volume they will reach people and organizations both in the Pittsburgh region and beyond who may suffer from painful economic change. Our intent is that the findings and policy proposals set forth here will help households and institutions deal with the effects of that change, which continue to afflict many families and small communities in the 1990s.

David E. Epperson, Dean
School of Social Work
University of Pittsburgh

Preface

This book presents a case study of a school working with communities in times of economic and social distress. The School of Social Work at the University of Pittsburgh has for many years been actively involved in a variety of ways with the steel towns along the Monongahela River system in western Pennsylvania. In the early 1980s massive plant closings led to economic catastrophe for the area, and the effects have persisted into the 1990s. The book is intended to highlight a process begun formally by the school in 1984, called the River Communities Project, which involved the administration, many of the faculty, and students from undergraduate, master's, and doctoral academic programs. The process demonstrates one approach by which schools of social work can fulfill their missions of teaching, service, and research by joining forces with community residents and thereby deriving direct benefits for both educational and community participants.

The case study operates on two levels. The carefully documented story of the impact of the massive mill closings in the Pittsburgh region is presented through research pieces. This is a unique chronicle of an industrial economic catastrophe. The book uses action-oriented research projects to vividly illustrate the terrible damage done to individuals, families, communities, indeed an entire region, when an economic disaster of this magnitude strikes. The data also clearly shows how recovery escapes the mill towns long after the immediate crisis has passed. The tragedy is dramatized by the efforts of communities to struggle out of the devastation.

On another level the book narrates the activities of the school as it entered into problem-solving efforts with the communities. The school's engagement with the communities and the search for information on the extent of devastation began and followed a course familiar to any social worker: the problem-solving course. Initially, students and faculty sought to develop tentative information on the nature of the crisis at the community level. The effort was then broadened in an attempt to seek confirmation of the preliminary findings elsewhere. As a body of evidence began emerging, increased attention was also paid to gathering more generalizable data. Greater attention was also paid to examining possible solutions to problems and making programmatic and policy recommendations. Efforts were also undertaken to implement, and evaluate the implementation of, alternative solutions to problems at the community level.

In the course of this problem-identifying and -solving process, school personnel offered services to the communities by working with local agencies and groups as action researchers, facilitators, and coordinators. In so doing, the school administration, faculty, and student body enriched themselves as social workers. All gained valuable experience through direct participation with people struggling and working at the local level.

The central focus in this case study is on a regional tragedy, one that unfortunately has been equaled in many places in the United States. The crisis is viewed through the lens of social work students and researchers and their involvement in affected communities and institutions. The study has implications for social work interventions, particularly action-oriented social work research as a form of social work intervention.

The case study is a distillation of documented interaction between a school and an economically stricken community over a period of years. Through the River Communities Project, administrators, faculty, and students at the school collaborated with academic colleagues, community residents, local agencies, and other institutions in action research, community organization, and demonstration projects. Reports from the project are drawn upon to provide the illustrative material for the book. The individuals who conducted the research and related activities are identified in the book, but the two editors have been given the responsibility to select and condense the material to represent the several phases of the project. Putting the components in place, using abridged reports as examples of research activities, and demonstrating the relationships of each individual research and demonstration project to the whole are the work of the editors.

Martha Baum
Pamela Twiss

Acknowledgments

Our very warmest thanks go to Cheryl Bartko first and foremost. With infinite patience and kindness, Cheryl helped us through the vicissitudes of several major revisions of the manuscript. And with her wonderful taste and expertise, Cheryl has made the book at least look beautiful.

We also want to thank several colleagues for taking the trouble to read and offer advice on parts of the book-in-progress. Jim Cunningham and Kenn Kornick, who was at that time the representative of the Alumni Association in the School of Social Work, were especially helpful.

PART ONE:
THE DEVASTATION

Chapter 1

The Loss of "Big Steel" and the Consequences for the River Communities

After the dynamic open economy of the 1950s and 1960s, America's hegemony in economic affairs eroded. Global competition spurred by the accelerating pace of technological change and the restructuring of world economies found the United States faltering. The nation's workforce had been traumatized by these changes. Official unemployment figures revealed an unrelenting upward trend. Unemployment during the 1950s averaged 4.2 percent of the workforce, rising to 4.8 percent in the 1960s and 6.2 percent in the 1970s. By the late 1970s, unemployment in a nonrecession economy was 7 percent. In the 1980s average unemployment reached about 8 percent, almost twice that of the 1950s.

According to a special Census Bureau survey analyzed by the Bureau of Labor Statistics, between January 1979 and January 1984, 11.5 million workers lost jobs due to plant closings or relocations, elimination of positions, or work slowdowns (U.S. Congress, Office of Technology Assessment, 1986). Nearly half of these, 5.1 million, were displaced workers who had held their jobs for at least three years. Of the displaced workers, almost half were in manufacturing, which accounted for only 20 percent of the overall labor force. According to the results from the Census Bureau survey, the occupational group most at risk was machine operators, assemblers, and repairers, who constituted 22 percent of the displaced workers but only 7.5 percent of the workforce as a whole. Of all displaced workers, one-fourth were out of work for at least one year between 1979 and 1984. When these workers were reemployed, survey data indicate, 45 percent had taken a pay cut, and two-thirds of the workers who had taken a pay cut were earning less than 80 percent of their former incomes. Although women and blacks were not over represented among displaced workers, they experienced significantly greater hardships in finding reemployment.

The national picture was bleak, but Pittsburgh, which lies in a county of more than one million people, was dealt an especially severe blow. It had had a rich base of industrial jobs, but Pittsburgh came out of the 1970s aging and in decline. In the 1980s the principal industry collapsed, and a large proportion of the region's households suffered through painful change. In the 1990s Pittsburgh is still struggling to recover, possessing large pockets of poverty and distress side by side with new economic engines of service and high technology whose reliability is yet to be tested.

For more than one hundred years prior to 1980, the Pittsburgh region was renowned as one of the world's great centers of heavy manufacturing. Numerous small communities developed around the large industrial plants that dominated the riverfronts, and enormous wealth was amassed from the creativity and labor of the residents. Monuments to this wealth are still visible today in the form of libraries, art collections, towering office buildings, mansions of faded elegance, philanthropic foundations, universities, and hospitals.

Though industry brought great wealth to the region, as well as a century of preeminence in steel production, economic recession was not unknown in Pittsburgh. Workers and their families experienced cycles of unemployment and recovery. The cycles created a climate in which workers viewed slowdowns and layoffs as both endemic and temporary. Pittsburghers were not prepared for the realities of the permanent shutdowns that occurred in the late 1970s and especially the early 1980s. By 1980, low-cost foreign steel, manufactured in ultramodern plants, was making heavy inroads into Pittsburgh markets. The comparative advantage of Pittsburgh markets was wiped out, bringing a massive wave of layoffs and plant closings to once prosperous mill towns and industrial neighborhoods. The basic steel industry in the previous decade, even though declining, had been responsible for more than 10 percent of total regional employment and approximately 16 percent of total payroll. In the wake of the 1980-1983 recession, steel accounted for less than 5 percent of employment and less than 9 percent of payroll (Bangs and Singh, 1990)

In the national picture as well the steel industry was doing poorly, with an estimated shutdown of more than 500 plants between 1974 and late 1985 (Thompson, 1985). The causes of the shutdowns were argued from many viewpoints but all seemed to agree that excess global capacity in the 1980s was central to the demise of steel in the United States. In an article in *Industry Week* J. Bruce Johnston, a U.S. Steel executive, stated: "The transcendent reality, dominating everything for both companies and the union, is the fact that the world now has more than 300 million tons of excess steel capacity. . . Eighty-four nations now make steel" (Johnston, as quoted in Thompson, 1985, p. 43).

The "transcendent reality" of overcapacity placed Pittsburgh steelworkers in a new and frightening situation. For the first time in this century, people faced layoffs that appeared to be permanent. The mills might not reopen. The once employable blue-collar workers could well find that their skills were obsolete and unmarketable in a changing economy. Their families faced the same uncertainties. Family incomes could fall permanently, and workers' plans for their own and their children's futures would fall with them. Community tax bases would necessarily spiral downward, leaving school districts, police forces, and basic municipal services in jeopardy. The blow would fall hardest in those communities that grew up along the rivers beside the mills, for their economic existence had been previously most tightly tied to steel and to the industries associated with steel. It is these mill towns and neighborhoods in most jeopardy that became the central focus and concern of the River Communities Project. The next chapter describes a preliminary research project in a stricken mill town.

Chapter 2

The Crisis at the Community Level: Exploring Aliquippa, 1984 and Before

Professor James Cunningham, a faculty member at the University of Pittsburgh School of Social Work who specializes in community organization, was responsible for teaching an organizational behavior course in the early 1980s. The students were searching for a group project they could undertake. They decided to examine what had been and was then occurring in the mill town of Aliquippa in the wake of two massive layoffs at its large LTV Steel plant. The central purpose behind studying Aliquippa flowed from the general purposes of social work research: develop knowledge that will benefit people, improve social work practices, and ameliorate human suffering (Rubin and Babbie, 1993). As one student in the class wrote of the final report on their project: "It is hoped that there are a few pieces of information and ideas in here that will help people and organizations survive right now, in 1984" (Blocher, 1984, p. 5).

Professor Cunningham and a group of students* did the research and the report from which the following findings are taken. The report, titled *Aliquippa: Struggle for Survival in a Pittsburgh Milltown, 1984 and Before*, was broadly disseminated. The following is a brief representation of what was learned in the process.

In selecting the mill town of Aliquippa, the class capitalized upon both the community's characteristics and the strengths of the mature

---

*The research team for the Aliquippa study included graduate students Elizabeth Blocher, Cathy A. Cairns, C. Matthew Hawkins, Robina Linear, Celestine Robb, Cheryl Trotter, and Joe Witherspoon. The final report was edited by Elizabeth Blocher, Cathy A. Cairns, James V. Cunningham, and C. Matthew Hawkins.

learners within the class. As Elizabeth Blocher, one of the students, wrote:

> Aliquippa was selected because of its economic condition. Hit hard by recession, it is a traditional milltown built around the predominant presence of the mill. The effects of a dying regional steel industry can be readily examined in such a town, one that is economically dependent on an industry on its downswing. The size of the community selected for study was another important consideration. Because it was the group's intent to study a community from an organizational perspective, it had to be large enough to have developed its own institutions and organizations. (Blocher, 1984, p. 4)

The selection of Aliquippa was also strongly supported by a member of the class, Cathy Cairns, who covered Aliquippa as a journalist and lived in the area. She was already familiar with the community's institutions and leadership and was able to help other members of the class to gain access to information and resources.

As noted by Blocher above, the class chose to examine Aliquippa through a particular lens: they looked at the community through its institutions and organizations. Students fanned out within the borough to separately look at religious bodies, organs of government, media, local businesses, and informal networks of support. They interviewed residents, local business owners, those working in the community, and those elected to represent the community. They attended public meetings. They also examined existing reports and statistics. All of this activity was focused upon addressing a series of questions:

> What mechanisms of survival have been brought into play in Aliquippa? Is it still functioning as a community? What are the strengths of the community and what are its weaknesses? Is there a willingness on the part of community leaders, institutions and individual residents to work together to develop coping strategies and to find solutions to the tough problems facing Aliquippa? Are Aliquippa and its people surviving, and if so, how? (Blocher, 1984, pp. 4-5)

The study was exploratory in nature, seeking preliminary and tentative findings upon which further investigations might be built. The students and their professor, in writing about their work, made no pretense of offering representative survey findings that were generalizable to a broad population. Their exploration, nevertheless, yielded dramatic results. Unemployment was not a new topic of inquiry, but an examination of the impact of massive unemployment upon an entire community, with the community serving as the unit of analysis, was not typical of studies of economic crisis.

The students found Aliquippa and its residents struggling to survive in 1984 and facing an extremely uncertain future. Located approximately 26 miles from Pittsburgh, on the Ohio River, Aliquippa was once a company town dominated by a steel mill that spanned six miles of riverfront property. Its history was intimately associated with the Jones and Laughlin Steel Company, from the early 1900s on. The community's neighborhoods were planned and established by a subsidiary of the Jones and Laughlin company. There was a company-affiliated department store that allowed charges against a steelworker's next paycheck. The library in the community's center had been donated by the daughter of B. F. Jones, a founder of J and L Steel Corporation. Aliquippa's ties to Jones and Laughlin brought prosperity for the better part of a century (with the exception of the Great Depression).

In the post-World War II era, demand for steel kept the local economy relatively strong. The growth of surrounding suburbs drained population from Aliquippa between 1960 and 1980, which detrimentally affected tax revenues and services, but the community was far from destroyed. As one student noted in studying the community: "While the current crisis striking Aliquippa is but one consequence of social and technological change underway in the region for more than 50 years, the size, suddenness, and intensity of this crisis is unusual" (Blocher, 1984, p. 3).

The changes wrought in the early 1980s were indeed intense and sudden. C. Matthew Hawkins, one of the students in the class, focused upon the borough's economic problems and their effects upon people. Utilizing existing reports and documents, he noted that although Aliquippa's steel mill had once employed 14,000 workers, it had only 3,500 at the time of the study, yet was still the principal employer. Two layoffs of massive proportions in 1982 (in February and June) had left many unemployed and facing the expiration of their unemployment compensation in 1984 (Hawkins, 1984).

Population as well as employment was declining. At the time of the study, it appeared that the borough was entering a critical period, one in which things would either stabilize and improve or continue spiralling downward. Students found residents and businesspeople alike wondering what the future would bring. The huge mill's parent company (now LTV Steel rather than Jones and Laughlin) merged with Republic Steel, bringing together under the same management two steelmaking facilities in the same county (Beaver County, Pennsylvania) that duplicated each other's efforts. Assurances were made by LTV Steel that the merger would not result in the closure of the Aliquippa facility. That did not quiet concerns, however. One restaurant owner was quoted as saying, "The town is about dead and will get worse. J and L will finally close. There's only 2400 jobs left there now" (Cunningham, 1984, p. 96).

By examining the community's institutions and organizations, the students found that further complicating any and all efforts of Aliquippa's residents to survive were social and political problems of long duration, particularly race relations and weak political institutions. In a community in which a third of the population was black, there was initially little (and later *no)* representation of blacks on the borough council. Relations between police and residents in the black neighborhoods were so poor that the frustrated local NAACP finally sought the aid of the Justice Department and the State's Attorney General to redress community grievances (Robb, 1984). The Democratic Party held sway, but Democrats elected to the borough council were involved in intraparty fights that prevented unified action on behalf of the community. They sought to govern with dramatically dwindling revenues, squeezed out of taxpayers with fewer and fewer dollars to spare.

A brief examination of the data that the students gathered on local government and school district revenues clarifies the extent of the budget crisis faced by borough council members. Between 1981 and 1983, the borough's wage tax revenue fell by $265,105 (from $480,282 in 1981 to $215,177 in 1983). The borough's total revenues dropped by nearly half a million dollars ($482,931), from

$2,737,716 in 1981 to $2,254,785 in 1983 (Cunningham, 1984, p. 86). The Aliquippa school district (which is coterminous with the borough) saw wage tax revenue drop from $403,021 in 1980-81 to $277,421 in 1982-83–a drop of $125,600–as unemployment rose.

Revenue losses were exacerbated when LTV Steel pursued and won reassessment of its enormous mill site. The borough had always been able to count on substantial tax income from the mill, and the reassessment pushed the borough to increase the already high tax burden on other property owners at a time of high unemployment, decreased wages, and diminished consumer demand.

At the end of their foray into Aliquippa, the class was prepared to address, at least tentatively, the questions of what the town had become and what its future might hold. That Aliquippa was still functioning as a community, with strengths and weaknesses, was evident. Its most dramatic weaknesses appeared to be the social and political fragmentation that threatened to pull the community into warring camps, with racial disharmony leading to the NAACP's efforts to seek external assistance in remedying the problems before they got worse. Economic crisis seemed only to exacerbate the tensions in the community and the weaknesses and paralysis of local government.

In terms of strengths, the students uncovered residents, local businesspeople, and leaders willing to commit themselves to the pursuit of a brighter future for Aliquippa. There was an organizational and social infrastructure, what is frequently referred to as "social fabric," that was yet maintained. And they found some survival mechanisms in informal support networks and in local social and religious bodies. "Support networks of kin, friends, neighbors, churches, social organizations, local financial institutions, and the like appear to have a key role in survival" (Blocher et al., 1984, p. 99).

The editors of the final report on the Aliquippa study concluded that those willing to work for Aliquippa's future needed to come together and build an organization that represented Aliquippa in its broadest sense to fight for the community's interests. "Since borough government's energy has been absorbed by internal political competition and by growing debts, the leadership for a comprehensive effort would most likely come from a broad community task force which would have leaders from all of the active groups" (Blocher et al., 1984, p. 101). One of the students undertook implementation of this recommendation and built the Aliquippa Alliance for Unity and Development, an effort described later in this book.

The editors also concluded that further research was necessary to shore up the tentative conclusions they had drawn from interviews with residents. They were particularly concerned with learning how social networks were helping people in the context of economic crisis. They concluded by calling for more scientific surveys to address questions related to household survival, particularly related to nutrition, shelter, health care, labor force entry and temporary jobs, retraining, emigration, human service utilization, and organizational and institutional interventions.

Most of the students in Professor Cunningham's class went on to complete their graduate educations and moved into the workforce without further contact with Aliquippa and its residents. However, for some of the students, and for the School of Social Work itself, the Aliquippa project was the beginning of a new effort to understand and try to intervene in the economic and social crisis being visited upon the region.

The report on the class effort, titled *Aliquippa: Struggle for Survival in a Pittsburgh Milltown, 1984 and Before*, was published in 1984 by the School of Social Work at the University of Pittsburgh, in cooperation with the University Center for Social and Urban Research. Findings from the report were broadly circulated. However, satisfying though that was for the students and others involved, it was not enough for many. The demise of steel was affecting other communities in the region. The massive layoffs were unprecedented in the post-Depression era. At the time the report was published, it was unclear what would happen to Aliquippa. It was unclear whether what the students found in Aliquippa was typical of other mill towns and communities in the region.

Professor Cunningham and other faculty within the school wanted to pursue the recommendations of the students and broaden the commitment of the school to researching the effects of massive plant closings on the communities and mill towns of the broader Pittsburgh region. As a first step, they sought verification that what had happened in Aliquippa was not completely unique to Aliquippa and that the findings were replicable in other communities within the region.

Simultaneously, students were supported and encouraged, through their field placements, in efforts to develop organizations to help struggling mill towns. As adult learners, they frequently brought the ideas for their placements to the school, at once influencing the communities they cared about and drawing the school further into commitments to distressed communities.

PART TWO:
EVOLUTION OF THE RIVER
COMMUNITIES PROJECT

Chapter 3

Steps in the Process

PROLOGUE

The social work perspective is a problem-solving perspective (Zastrow, 1985). When confronted with a problem, be it at the individual, community, or societal level, social workers seek to solve the problem. This orientation pervades all activity within the field. Social work research is set apart from other social research by its orientation. Rather than seeking knowledge for its own sake, social work research seeks to alleviate human suffering and to inform social work practice and social welfare policy (Rubin and Babbie, 1993).

Zastrow sets forth the following as the steps in the social work problem-solving approach:

1. Identify as precisely as possible the problem or problems.
2. Generate possible alternative solutions.
3. Evaluate the alternative solutions.
4. Select a solution or solutions to be used, and set goals.
5. Implement the solution(s).
6. Follow up to evaluate how the solution(s) worked. (Zastrow, 1985, p. 15)

Given this orientation to problem solving, it was most natural for the School of Social Work to seek to first understand and then develop programmatic and policy solutions to the economic crisis that enveloped the Pittsburgh region in the early 1980s. The chapters that follow present in case study form one school's efforts to respond to an emergency.

The response unfolded naturally along the lines of typical social work efforts. Initially, social work students working with faculty sought an understanding of the crisis at the community level. In response to their dramatic findings, faculty and administrators developed a more organized research agenda. This agenda began with efforts to seek confirmation of the preliminary findings at the community level across a broader spectrum of the affected area. As patterns emerged across communities, efforts were undertaken to explore and describe, in increasingly systematic ways, the differential impacts on various population groups.

In the midst of data gathering, indeed beginning very early in the exploratory work, students and faculty also began developing programmatic initiatives to be tested in communities where plant closings had occurred. Plans were also initiated to evaluate these preliminary attempts to find solutions.

Throughout the process, much was learned about the interactions of community and school, community and university. The lessons were not all positive. This book closes with chapters devoted to examining relations between the school and the communities and organizations touched by the research and problem-solving efforts. It is hoped that other schools, universities, and social work students and faculty can use this information to bring the resources of academic settings to struggling communities in increasingly positive ways and with greater understanding and sensitivity.

HISTORICAL INVOLVEMENT WITH THE MILL TOWNS AND THE USE OF THE CONCEPT OF COMMUNITY

This book presents a carefully documented response of a school of social work to economic disaster in neighboring communities. When the steel industry left southwestern Pennsylvania, it took with it not only the steelworking jobs but also the giant's share of other jobs in a number of towns where steel had been king. The School of Social Work at the University of Pittsburgh acted slowly at first, testing the waters, so to speak, to see how much damage had been done, and then moved more formally and comprehensively in a structured process of investigation.

The project format that was developed reflects to some extent integrated social work processes in which research, community organization, and social action were interwoven. The approach appears well suited to the development of a comprehensive understanding of communities in pain. The River Communities Project arose in response to economic catastrophe in towns and neighborhoods with which the school had long been familiar. In an era of plant closings, deindustrialization, declining per capita income, persistent unemployment and underemployment, and attendant social problems, economic issues have been given top priority in many parts of the United States. They were of central concern in this project also, although inevitably human service workers were concerned with the social and emotional consequences of economic collapse as well.

The school has been involved with the river communities since its founding. The students served in placements in their agencies and received the benefits of the supervising expertise of the professionals in those agencies. In turn, our faculty and administrators were deeply involved in community service, sitting on agency boards, consulting with agency personnel about service delivery, offering assistance on research techniques such as needs assessment and practice evaluation, and training personnel to work with special populations (such as the elderly) and populations with special needs (such as AIDS victims). With so much reciprocal contact, school members could not avoid becoming aware of the distress as the withdrawal of steel progressed. But the first evidence of the depth and endurance of distress in the region was gathered piecemeal, in very small studies carried out by school faculty or collected from comments and insights gathered from practitioners, students in internships, and through agency visits.

There were no systematic data available on the towns in the area. Labor market data were not helpful in terms of determining the extent of unemployment, since the populations of many river communities were too small to be included in the monthly reports of the Bureau of Labor Statistics. The 1980 U.S. census was too early to hint at the impact of the massive shutdowns of 1981 and 1982. If anything, damage was underestimated in what reports became available. The severest layoffs had occurred by the mid-1980s, and many "outsiders" assumed that the river communities were in the process of recovery.

But one-industry towns, particularly isolated one-industry towns, do not recover easily, as would be discovered. When the larger survey, described in Chapter 8, was conducted in Aliquippa, the results led the school to become far more actively engaged.

Before this book proceeds, however, the use of the term "community" in this context deserves brief consideration. The traditional use of the word "community" is often misapplied in common parlance, at least with reference to place. The essence of community has to do with social interaction among residents (Martinez-Brawley, 1990). Community relationships are closely knit and enduring. Residents have a clear understanding of where each person stands in the social schema. Values and norms are shared and constantly reinforced by face-to-face interaction. Peaceful, cooperative social ties are characteristic of true communities. Perhaps it is a nostalgia in urban settings for small-town ambiance that brings about the overuse of the term "community" in the United States. The one-industry, often geographically segregated, small enclaves that constituted the mill towns were referred to and perceived by many to be communities, but the apparent social cohesion was fragile. Severe stress, as in the face of economic disaster, leads people to find mutual cooperation and support difficult. Cleavages that previously went more or less unnoticed become sharply defined in a crisis. So-called communities find themselves divided by social class and ethnic-racial ties. This is what happened in many of the mill towns, and it made the townspeople's struggles to overcome tragedy even more problematic. In discussing the River Communities Project, the term "community" is often used, although the appropriateness of its use is subject to reservations, as just expressed.

THE SCHOOL AND THE RIVER COMMUNITIES PROJECT: MAKING A FORMAL COMMITMENT

The project really acquired momentum when the graduate class in organizational behavior produced a report on its findings on Aliquippa after the steel industry departed. The results described in the report were so appalling that they received prime local newspaper coverage and were even the subject of a feature article in *The New York Times*. Aliquippa was a one-company town with the enormous steel mill dominating community life and blocking out any other sizable business enterprises. This was a common situation in the river communities. Aliquippa was viewed by those carrying out the research, and by community residents as well, as a microcosm reflecting the southwestern Pennsylvania region as a whole. It was also recognized, however, that Aliquippa was even more isolated than most river towns, and that there was a need to find out how other communities in the region were faring before decisions about further action were made. The study of Aliquippa at least destroyed the sanguine belief that the river communities were in recovery.

The result was that the school "went formal" with what was called the River Communities Project. A structure was developed, goals were outlined, specific targets were chosen, and start-up funds were solicited. As the project unfolded, the applicability of the process to other places suffering through troubled times became apparent. Accordingly, great care has been taken to describe the elements that were initiated, expanded, and eventually pulled together as project efforts. The project description furnishes examples that highlight the process and demonstrate the choices made along the way, the rationale for such choices, and their contributions to the whole.

The Dean of the school, David E. Epperson, played a strong leadership role as the project's director, with Professor James Cunningham serving as principal investigator and constant vital spark plug for the project. Associate Dean Tony Tripodi and key faculty became involved in a number of capacities, including designing and carrying out action-oriented research projects, serving as community-organizing consultants and facilitators, sitting on the advisory board, and chipping in as authors and editors. Other faculty were available to offer helpful advice, ideas, and other assistance. Students were into everything from library searches to interviewing and observing to coding data and writing reports. Master's and doctoral students sometimes played major roles in the design and implementation of research projects and in conducting evaluations of demonstration efforts. Even members of the school who did not become directly engaged learned about what was going on through classroom presentations and lunchtime seminars. The commitment of the school was exceptional, even though in many instances this meant finding ways to donate time despite already crowded schedules, for, in spite of unceasing efforts to obtain financial assistance, money was always tight. Tight money also meant that some desirable proposed projects never became realities.

A legion of people were ultimately involved in the project, and all of their names cannot be mentioned. Those who made major contributions are, of course, credited as their efforts are described in the text. Members of the University community outside the school became involved as individual faculty or in administrative capacities and contributed to the River Communities Project, as did many people working in the Pittsburgh region in various organizations and roles. What the school gained from others, both within and outside the University of Pittsburgh, is acknowledged as the narrative moves along. Collaboration was essential to carrying out the River Communities Project, even though the major initiative came from the school.

The first step toward designing and implementing the project was to set up a management structure. In the case of the River Communities Project, an executive committee was formed to guide the process. The committee included the Dean, the Associate Dean, six faculty and three staff members from the school with diverse interests and skills, and the Director of the University of Pittsburgh's Center for Social and Urban Research. The six faculty members were appointed to the executive committee by the Dean and represented about one-fifth of the full-time faculty. At least another quarter of the faculty participated in subprojects. The executive committee met, at a minimum, twice a month. During periods of high activity, which were frequent, they met more often. The membership of the executive committee remained quite stable throughout the research phases, although meetings frequently included other members of the school and colleagues from other parts of the University who were active in ongoing projects.

The executive committee was charged with the following responsibilities:

* Plan overall strategy.
* Establish policy guidelines.
* Review work in progress.
* Approve reports for binding and dissemination.

- Approve changes in project budgets and methodology.
- Keep the University community, the project's funders, and those in the Pittsburgh region informed about the project.

Meeting biweekly and inviting other interested members of the school and the university to participate, the committee managed to fulfill all of these responsibilities. Perhaps the most important task of all was the mandate to put together a proposal for funding for a second phase of the project, using results from the four exploratory studies that were carried out following the first Aliquippa research.

As the committee pursued its work, in constant consultation with colleagues, graduate students, and community leaders and residents, the overall major goals of the River Communities Project were formulated, as listed below:

1. To conduct a rigorous investigation of social concerns in the devastated communities of the Pittsburgh region, with small communities, families, and local institutions as the units of analysis;
2. To advance knowledge and understanding of the human consequences of the severe social and economic changes now unsettling older urban regions;
3. To develop and carry out relevant demonstrations with the people and institutions of these communities;
4. To advance the educational and skills training of student social workers by their participation in the project;
5. To identify the principal issues and to formulate useful and feasible public policy recommendations;
6. To publish and disseminate findings through books, articles, reports, mass media, press conferences, classroom instruction, workshops, and seminars.

THE PHASES OF THE PROJECT

In the project's initial phase of executive committee meetings (to which Parts One and Two of this book offer introductory information), broad principles of purpose were laid down as listed in the preceding paragraph. Each subsequent phase of the project was developed according to those principles, yet responsive to the experiences of the preceding phase. The first action phase of the project, which is discussed in Part Three, was perceived as an information-building effort that would extend and enhance the preliminary findings from Aliquippa. From the beginning, it was anticipated that the school's activities would produce additional efforts such as community coalitions and demonstration projects. Colleagues in other parts of the University were encouraged to participate. The projects launched by the school, if successful in arousing interest and a desire to assist area revival, would, in turn, produce unplanned efforts. Although this sounds unstructured, the strategy adopted depended on the school's projects to catch fire in the affected communities.

There is necessarily some uncertainty about exactly what will happen in a flexible setup that is open to, and encouraging of, new endeavors. Community people were therefore sought out and encouraged to help the school probe into areas of local concern so that fruitful action-oriented research could be initiated. In the project, therefore, the executive committee set the basic agenda, based upon what was known and what needed to be known; but what actually took place was not entirely predictable. Uncertainty was acceptable because of the desire to work with the community as far as possible, following leads obtained from residents, local leaders, business owners–indeed, anyone concerned. Once the extent and duration of the economic damage began to be known, many individuals, groups, organizations, and institutions became involved.

Knowledge was produced through action-oriented research initiated by the school. Action-oriented research consists of the systematic gathering of essential information by those who are affected by a social problem and by those who want to solve it (Waltz and Groze, 1991). In effect the two groups are intermingled to a large extent, as was the case with mill town residents and social worker researchers. It follows that research of this type is not necessarily value-neutral, or "clean," in the sense that it does not distinguish the findings from the people affected. Action-oriented research does not seek knowledge only for its own sake, but links research to social change. Social scientists carrying out action-oriented research can find natural allies in the community to help in collecting, analyzing, and, perhaps especially, interpreting data.

One important use of such data is to promote community organization and planning efforts.

The first phase of the River Communities Project was perceived as an exploratory information building effort which would extend the preliminary project findings. The Aliquippa study was the first large-scale inquiry to look at a mill town community as a whole after the collapse of the steel industry. Jim Cunningham, who became the principal investigator for the entire River Communities Project, and his students met with knowledgeable community people who could guide them in conducting a study that encompassed the key community variables. The Aliquippa research disclosed a deep social tragedy.

The first phase of the project set out to answer two questions related to the Aliquippa findings: Were other towns and neighborhoods in the area similarly affected? Were there differences in the experiences of different population groups within or across localities? The executive committee agreed that projects needed to be carried out in several other river communities, and that it would be important to interview both community leaders and samples of residents. The first phase was exploratory, oriented to assessing the generality of economic catastrophe, as well as factors that tended to vary from locality to locality. Four projects were undertaken, supported by seed funding for the River Communities Project proposal that was developed by the executive committee; these projects are discussed in Chapters 4 through 7. One, titled *Aliquippa Update,* used secondary data and interviews with targeted informants in that community to reassess the town two years after the initial study. Three additional local areas were also studied. Community leaders and broad samples of residents were interviewed. The last two of the four studies ("The Triborough Study" and "Duquesne") were the most systematic in sampling and breadth of coverage. The Triborough study had, for the first time, research participation beyond the school. It involved political scientists who, in cooperation with the Graduate School of Public and International Affairs at the University of Pittsburgh, carried out a project in a tripartite locality suffering long-term economic decline; the River Communities Project published and distributed a technical document that included their report.

The second phase of the project, described in Part Four, built upon the information gathered in the exploratory phase and proceeded to a more mature research phase. The executive committee developed a plan to advance understanding of the massive changes affecting people and communities, to clarify key issues, and to move closer to the development of micro and macro policy to address critical problems. Much of the mature phase work was devoted to fleshing out the knowledge base through in-depth studies on specific role and household configurations identified in the exploratory research as needing closer attention. A special feature of the in-depth studies was a focus on those factors across and within particular types of households that would provide targets for intervention and be linked to policy considerations. The more-in-depth research was conducted in some of the mill town areas already studied and in several additional ones. The results from these studies are integrated in the summary.

Across the four projects, a concern with race was manifest. Earlier it was mentioned that communities with severe problems often become divided within themselves. Across the river communities, many animosities sprang up between groups. Resentment against executives and managers of the mills was high. Sentiment for and against the unions caused divisions. People in some places felt that their particular residential area was unfairly slighted when it came to alleviating poverty and distributing job training. Already in the exploratory research, however, it became apparent that the main line of antagonism in the river communities was between blacks and whites. African-Americans are, by far, the largest racial minority in the region, and significant numbers of blacks lived in some of the mill towns. The first-phase studies revealed that this group was the hardest hit by the loss of jobs. Blacks who were able to enter the steel industry, albeit late in its history, had been doing quite well, but now their seemingly secure foothold was gone. Black persons were struggling even harder than white persons and with less reward. Black-white antagonism could only be aggravated through the competition for jobs after the mills collapsed. Each of the studies carried out in the second phase included a large proportion of black respondents so that more in-depth information on this particular cleavage could be obtained and applied to policy and service considerations.

The last project phase, which is reported on in Part Five, crosses in time both the first and second phases. Unexpectedly early in the exploratory phase of the project, major developments emerged in the form of self-help groups in several communities. The school provided some start-up funds and expert assistance for selected efforts and obtained documented assessments in return. One self-help project reported on in Part Five was the Aliquippa Alliance for Unity and Development, which was organized by a master's student in the school. She continued her efforts beyond the beginnings and eventually established a full-fledged, multifaceted community institution. Two other students helped to develop the Homestead Community Credit Union, a much more specifically pinpointed organizing effort. One of these students went on to initiate the Mon Valley Development Team, a planning operation that eventually spread throughout the area and to other parts of the country. These projects are included in this book because they illustrate more fully the tensions that had to be dealt with before people could begin working together to attempt to find solutions to their problems.

Demonstration projects stemming from the action research developed later in the span of the project but are included as part of this mixed-time third phase. As results were reviewed across communities, the most pervasive and poignant problem identified was the out-migration of youth. Together with local institutions, private foundations, local community leaders, and young people, the school joined forces to mount a youth enterprise project in one river community; eventually projects were set up in three communities. These youth demonstration projects illustrate the very serious problems in implementing anything substantial and long-term in financially devastated communities with many pressing needs.

The final chapter in Part Five describes the presentation of results from all three project phases. The presentations were given in a number of well-publicized seminars held both at the University and in the various communities affected by the economic catastrophe. The well-attended seminars provided a forum for community members to respond to the research, offer additional input, and suggest new directions. The seminars provided a fitting conclusion to the action stages of the River Communities Project and a bridge to the more contemplative stages of rethinking the project and of policy discussion.

Rethinking the project takes place in Part Six. These final chapters look back at the River Communities Project in several ways and also offer some up-to-date information on the status of the mill towns in 1993, some ten years after the first research was conducted. The methodology of the project is subjected to a brief critical analysis with special attention to school-community relations and to assessing the gains and risks in joint ventures between a school and its external community.

The most prominent discussion in Part Six centers on making use of the knowledge gained from project activities, first at the micro policy level and then at the macro policy level. The limits of community self-help in a widespread economic disaster are carefully examined, using a case study of a community organization that was especially versatile in coordinating group activities and attracting financial and other resources. Two popular macro legislative attempts, one at the federal and one at the state level, designed to alleviate economic stress, are also described. In the conservative socioeconomic climate of the 1980s, however, public interventions requiring large sums of money did not materialize.

Finally, some last words on the project are presented, beginning with an update of a six-community systematic study that allows a comparison between the circumstances of the people in those mill towns in 1989 and in 1993. Although 1993 brought to an official end the River Communities Project, a new thrust that was designed from its findings has taken place. This thrust is discussed and supplemented by an interview with the principal investigator of the River Communities Project, Professor James Cunningham.

PART THREE:
EXPLORATORY RESEARCH:
SEEKING CONFIRMATION
AT THE COMMUNITY LEVEL

In 1985 the Pittsburgh Foundation, a community foundation, provided seed money to the University of Pittsburgh's School of Social Work to start the River Communities Project (RCP). The initial seed funding for the project was to support three efforts closely linked to the Aliquippa study: a follow-up study of Aliquippa, a study of several communities dependent upon the production of electricity and steel (hereafter frequently referred to as the "Electric Valley"), and a broad survey of households in Duquesne, a mill town in Pittsburgh's Monongahela Valley. Early in the life of the River Communities Project, it was agreed that seed funds would also be used to publish a uniquely compatible study undertaken by a professor and two students in the Political Science department and the Graduate School of Public Affairs of the University of Pittsburgh. This study of the Triborough area–the boroughs of Braddock, North Braddock, and Rankin–added a fourth study to the exploratory phase.

The structure and functions of the Aliquippa and the Electric Valley studies were very similar to those of the original Aliquippa study. They focused upon whole communities as units of analysis. The Duquesne study, by contrast, focused upon individual households and household members as units of analysis and represented the school's first effort to develop a representative sample of households affected by the massive layoffs in the region. The Triborough study focused primarily upon three geographically and socially related communities–Braddock, North Braddock, and Rankin–as a single unit of analysis. The study also included analyses of secondary data at the borough level, and included a representative sample of household members as well as a sample of local leaders. The use of multiple units of analysis, multiple sources of data, and social science survey methods made the Triborough study an excellent contribution to this phase of research.

Each of the three studies actually carried out by the School of Social Work was designed to build upon the initial exploration of Aliquippa and the recommendations that resulted from that first study. The questions that the students involved in the Aliquippa study proposed for further, more systematic investigation, for example, established the framework for further inquiry: How were families and households surviving? How were people finding food, shelter, and jobs?

Were people seeking help from organizations and institutions and, if so, were they being helped?

Again, the questions and the studies pursued were geared not only to knowledge building, but also to the traditional social work pursuit of problem solving. The Triborough study, while designed outside of the School of Social Work, was strikingly well suited to addressing these questions and to helping to solve problems as well.

As each study began and unfolded, concern continued to center upon potential policies and programs to help ameliorate the effects of economic and social crisis upon people, families, households, and communities and their institutions. Toward the end of this period in which researchers sought to confirm the first Aliquippa study's findings elsewhere, increased emphasis began to be placed upon the second step in the problem-solving process: generating possible alternative solutions to the problems. In the sections that follow, the four separate studies and their findings are discussed in some detail.

Chapter 4

Aliquippa Update

Aliquippa's industrial heritage and history are unique. A brief summary of Aliquippa's ties to steelmaking is included in Part One, and readers are encouraged to review that material, which is not presented again here to avoid repetition. The follow-up study of Aliquippa, called *Aliquippa Update,* was conducted in 1986, two years after the first study. In 1986 the nation appeared to be enjoying the beginnings of an economic recovery. The official national unemployment rate dropped from a high of 10.8 percent in 1983 to 7 percent in 1986. Beaver County, Pennsylvania, the county in which Aliquippa is situated, by contrast, dropped from an official unemployment rate of 23.1 percent in February of 1983 to 14 percent in early 1986. While declines in unemployment are good news, the drop in Beaver County still left behind double-digit unemployment. Further, there was cause to believe that the drop was not attributable to real decreases in unemployment. Rather, decreases in the number of people actively seeking work (with discouraged workers falling out of the counts and young people leaving to seek jobs elsewhere) cut the size of the civilian labor force (Cairns and Cunningham, 1986, p. 37).

Between 1980 and 1986, manufacturing employment in Beaver County dropped from 35,300 jobs to 16,100, a loss of 19,200 jobs, of which 9,000 were located in Aliquippa, Beaver County's largest municipality. Residents of Aliquippa held an estimated 1,800 of the 9,000 jobs lost in Aliquippa (Cairns and Cunningham, 1986, p. 35). Not surprisingly, given these figures, the team of researchers updating the earlier findings from Aliquippa found the community in much worse shape economically in 1986 than in 1984. Employment at the large steel mill continued to decline after 1983. Earned income tax receipts plummeted.

The researchers writing the *Aliquippa Update* report estimated, based upon unemployment figures for the surrounding county and upon school district wage receipts, that unemployment in Aliquippa in 1986 was over 30 percent, with residents holding approximately 3,700 full- and part-time jobs inside and outside of the community (of a potential civilian labor force of approximately 5,300). A 1986 survey undertaken of 512 households in one neighborhood plan within Aliquippa found an unemployment rate of 54 percent and a median household income of $16,300. The neighborhood surveyed had a reputation for being a "well kept, medium-income neighbor-hood populated largely by homeowners who are present or former steelworkers" (Cairns and Cunningham, 1986, p. 32).

When the 1984 study of Aliquippa was done, the borough had three major employers: the steel mill with 3,500 workers, the hospital with 576, and the railroad company with 300. In 1986, the researchers found employment at the steel mill down to 900, the hospital to 550, and the railroad to just 40 (Modany and Cunningham, 1986). The main street in Aliquippa, Franklin Avenue, now had many boarded store-fronts. There was no longer even a grocery store.

Still, the researchers found the community persisting and strug-gling. The informal networks of support continued. The religious and social organizations still provided some support to residents. Soup kitchens and food and clothing distribution were now the functions of a number of churches and organizations. Newer orga-nizations were emerging, as well, some to help with survival needs and others to organize for change for the future and to develop a unified voice for the community. Among these newer organizations were the Unemployed Committee of Beaver County and the Ali-quippa Alliance for Unity and Development. The latter organization was founded through the efforts of Cathy Cairns and many others in the community, and was in part a response to the identification of latent leadership and energy in the community uncovered through the first Aliquippa study (in which Cairns took part).

The *Aliquippa Update* study closed with the identification of a pattern of community response to crisis. At its most specific level, the pattern was identified as the phased response of institutions and organizations within the community. The researchers organized their findings to demonstrate this response as an unfolding process of essentially three phases: sheer survival, getting jobs, and, finally, a search for unity.

Organizations and institutions first concerned themselves with helping people to survive by assisting them to secure food, shelter, clothing, and other essentials for existence. Churches and self-help organizations were critical to these efforts.

Attention could then be paid to the business of job creation. Here the researchers found traditional economic development entities as well as newer organizations involving residents in planning for the future. Finally, there was recognition that in order to seek and gain attention from parties with resources (particularly state and federal levels of government), organization was needed to forge a unified vision of the community's future. Here, newer organizations worked with traditional forms, such as local government and social organizations of importance within the community, to seek and create unity.

The summary statement of the researchers for their 1986 report on Aliquippa was optimistic:

> The Aliquippa case indicates both the tragedy and hope of the small industrial community in the 1980's. Such communities are not going to regain their former glory and massive employment base. They are going to be smaller, with fewer jobs and people, and the people are going to be older. . . . [There are] in such communities family strengths and institutions capable of rebuilding a satisfying way of life, although a more austere one than that enjoyed during past years. (Cairns and Cunningham, 1986, p. 85)

The study indicated that in spite of yet further deterioration and misery, the community remained. Was Aliquippa special in this regard, or were these dynamics–the push for survival, job creation, and unity–at work in other mill towns and communities in the Pittsburgh region?

Chapter 5

The Electric Valley

Even as data were being gathered for the updated study of Aliquippa, another group of social work students,* in a research class with Professor James Cunningham, was exploring other communities. This time the students were studying two communities linked by their relationship with and dependence upon the production of electricity and steel. The two boroughs–East Pittsburgh and Turtle Creek–are referred to as the Electric Valley.

Prior to their industrial development, the communities that make up the Electric Valley were home to Native Americans and early farm settlements. Later the Valley was mined for coal and the production of rail for the railroads began providing jobs for many of the Valley's inhabitants. Braddock, a neighboring community, became the home of the Edgar Thomson Works, manufacturing rail in the late 1800s.

Efficient rail transport and manufacture in the area attracted George Westinghouse. Westinghouse's decision to locate large facilities in the Valley transformed the area and was the source of the Valley's prosperity for decades. In the years that followed, Andrew Carnegie's steel company expanded the Edgar Thomson Works in nearby Braddock while Westinghouse expanded in the Valley. The history of steel and electrical production in the area are linked to one another and, beginning with World War I, to warfare.

---

*The research team for the Electric Valley study included graduate students Margaret Chorpenning, Rita P. Costa, Randi Dobkin, Shannon Guy, Judy Ismail-Beigi, Anita Hrebinko, Peter Kelley, Barbara Kunschner, Richard L. Losasso, Susanne K. Miller, Charles H. Monsour, Stacy Moore, Jeff Morris, Willie E. McLendon, Carl Redwood, Jr., Barbara Sahlaney, Chaiw-Yi Shih, Carla R. Smith, Kay Snyder, Leanne Unites, Willie A. Wise, Jr., and James K. Yost. The final report was edited by James Cunningham and Pamela Martz.

Westinghouse, for example, produced explosive shells, radio receivers, and Russian military rifles for World War I. During World War II, manufacturing industries in the Turtle Creek Valley employed more than 50,000 (Department of Labor and Industry, 1983). The relationship of steel to war is discussed in the section that follows on Duquesne, Pennsylvania.

Following World War II, the Valley, like other areas heavily dependent upon industrial facilities, began to experience economic decline. Employment in industrial facilities fell to an average of 20,000 in the 1960s in the Turtle Creek Valley and was down to 14,000 in the 1970s (Department of Labor and Industry, 1983). The Valley's decline was of concern to planners in the late 1960s and efforts were undertaken to improve the social and economic conditions in the Valley.

Plans focused upon retaining the three industrial giants so important to the communities—the Edgar Thomson Works (U.S. Steel), Westinghouse Air Brake (later owned by American Standard Corporation), and the Westinghouse Electric Corporation—even though combined total employment was expected to continue to decline in the 1980s and 1990s. The plans for the future depended upon the continued investment of these corporations in their facilities and in the Valley. As the group of social work students began exploring the Valley, employment at Edgar Thomson was down to 700, and American Standard had announced the closing of the Westinghouse Air Brake facility. Westinghouse Electric, in East Pittsburgh, had lost more than 400 employees in the six months prior to the study.

STUDY METHODS

The focus for the students was again the community, with East Pittsburgh and the Turtle Creek Valley jointly being examined. The students fanned out into the community to gain information. This time they worked with a sponsoring organization and mentor, the Human Services Center Corporation, headed by executive director Tracy Soska.

Their inquiry involved both structured interviews and qualitative methods. Initially, students decided upon a specific area of inquiry (for example, health care, human services, and local government).

With the assistance of their community mentor, they then drew up lists of people important to the community whose work was related to their chosen area of interest. Each student then conducted interviews with approximately six of these leaders.

Students combined the information gathered from their interviews with data from existing sources to address the impact of unemployment and economic crisis upon their area of interest. They submitted reports to their professor in these areas. A subset of the initial class then took on the task of examining the reports and the combined data from all of the interviews and working with their professor to produce a final report. As gaps in information were identified, this subset of students made additional forays into the community to gather new data.

STUDY FINDINGS

Their findings did not perfectly mirror those of the students who studied Aliquippa. In studying the Electric Valley, the students were looking at communities in some ways dissimilar to Aliquippa. The communities of the Valley, while linked to the history of industrial giants, were not solely dependent upon production at one facility, although the several facilities were all declining. Examining the organizational and institutional structure of the Valley presented the students with additional complexities. Two municipalities rather than one were involved and the school district was a multicommunity district serving both relatively prosperous and poorer communities. The Valley also enjoyed greater proximity to both the City of Pittsburgh and its surrounding suburban communities.

The Valley also shared much with Aliquippa. Population loss was comparable. The combined communities of East Pittsburgh and the Turtle Creek Valley lost 41.4 percent of their population in 25 years; Aliquippa lost 43.9 percent of its population during the same period (Cunningham and Martz, 1986, p. 19). The Electric Valley, like Aliquippa, had witnessed population losses and economic decline prior to the 1980s and had then been thrown into rapid, dramatic economic crisis in the 1980s. The racial mix of the Valley was significantly different from that of Aliquippa, however, with the Valley being overwhelmingly Caucasian. One-third of Aliquippa's population, it will be remembered, was black at the time of the studies.

While the communities of the Electric Valley were not found to be as yet as distressed as the mill town of Aliquippa, the students found a great deal of evidence that the economic crisis hitting the Pittsburgh region was widespread. Manufacturing jobs in the Valley had declined from 50,000 in the 1940s to 20,000 in the 1960s; in the 1970s there were still 14,000 jobs but in the 1980s there were fewer than 5,000. In July 1986, when the students were completing their study, the Edgar Thomson Works, Westinghouse Air Brake, and the Westinghouse Electric facility in East Pittsburgh had lost many employees. Westinghouse Air Brake, in fact, was being shut down with a planned complete closing by 1987. Utilizing U.S. Census data, earned income tax receipts, and information on layoffs at nearby facilities, Cunningham and Martz estimated that the unemployment rate for the two boroughs in 1986 was approximately 15 percent, twice that of Allegheny County, the county in which the communities are located, for the same year (Cunningham and Martz, 1986, p. 20).

Job losses and plant shutdowns mean revenue losses for municipalities. Revenue losses invariably result in declining levels of government services. As in Aliquippa, the boroughs affected in the Electric Valley suffered dramatic revenue losses in the 1980s. The two boroughs combined lost approximately 50 percent of their revenue in constant dollars (Miller, 1986). The views expressed by the local leaders interviewed provided further evidence that the Valley's communities were indeed hard hit. Ninety-five percent of the Valley's local leaders viewed unemployment as a major problem affecting the people of the Valley. Eighty-eight percent of the local leaders believed that economic conditions had worsened in the three years prior to the study and 60 percent believed conditions would worsen in the next three years. Approximately 60 percent viewed the economic conditions of the Valley as poor, and 53 percent would have advised young people to leave the Valley to seek futures elsewhere at the time of the study (Cunningham and Martz, 1986).

At the close of the study of the Electric Valley, the students and their professor concluded that the three-phase response pattern identified in Aliquippa (survival, job creation, and a search for unity) was not replicated in the Electric Valley. The Valley had a rich set of organizations and institutions already established to assist households in meeting survival needs. Valley governments were already cooperating in councils of government and the Valley had been the recipient of significant government attention (including a Model Cities program). Yet there was a need for greater collaboration and a new collective vision of the Valley's future to which organizations and their supporters could attach their efforts.

The nature of the research in the Valley was still exploratory. From this preliminary work, however, new problems for attention emerged. The interviews with local leaders pointed to a dismal future for the Valley if the needs and futures of youth were not considered. The economy was sufficiently grim that more than half of the local leaders stated that they would advise youth to leave their hometown.

Chapter 6

The Triborough Study

As the community studies already discussed were being conducted and completed, Political Science Professor Michael Margolis
and graduate students Robert E. Burtt and Jeffrey McLaughlin
simultaneously carried out complementary work through another
department and school within the University of Pittsburgh. Their
target for study–the Triborough, comprised of Braddock, North
Braddock, and Rankin–the structure of their inquiry, and their
results so closely paralleled the work of the River Communities
Project that arrangements were made to publish their findings along
with the School of Social Work reports on other community studies.
Braddock, North Braddock, and Rankin sit within ten miles of Pittsburgh and share much of the geography and history of other mill
towns in the region. The Monongahela River outlines the communities on one side and provides the flatlands that led to wealth creation
and jobs production for generations here.

U.S. Steel's Edgar Thomson Works, or "ET," dominates Braddock's waterfront. The Edgar Thomson mill was opened in 1875.
With it came jobs and immigrants. Margolis, Burtt, and McLaughlin
note that within 30 years of the mill's opening (1900) the population
of the Triborough grew to 26 thousand, and 20 years later had
almost doubled, surpassing 43 thousand (Margolis, Burtt, and
McLaughlin, 1986, p. 11). The mix of immigrants flooding the
communities changed over time. The Triborough study states that
early waves of immigrants were from the British Isles and Ireland,
while the massive expansion of population in the early 1900s
involved a tremendous influx of southern and eastern European
Catholics; African Americans arrived in large numbers in 1919
(Margolis, Burtt, and McLaughlin, 1986, p. 13).

41

The immigrants who settled in the Triborough brought diversity and a cultural richness to the area and its civic life. Ethnic clubs and churches were developed. The Triborough became an economic hub for the wider region, with "the largest regional shopping district outside of Pittsburgh" in downtown Braddock (Margolis, Burtt, and McLaughlin, 1986, p. 13). The communities even survived the Depression of the 1930s well. As in some other communities, it was the post-World War II period that brought the first signs of real economic decline to the Triborough.

The industrial sites that generated jobs and wealth continued to prosper in the post-World War II era. Some mill workers, however, moved to the newly developing suburbs. By 1960 the population in the Triborough had declined from a peak of 44,066 in 1930 to 30,705, a drop of 30 percent. The decline was not stemmed at this point. Rather, in the years after 1960, the rate of population loss increased. Between 1960 and 1980, population dipped by another 13,000, yielding an overall decline, from 1930 to 1980, of greater than 60 percent. This decrease in population was particularly troublesome because the loss was not equally distributed across income groups. As Margolis, Burtt, and McLaughlin state: "Mostly, the richer whites moved out, leaving poorer whites and blacks behind" (Margolis, Burtt, and McLaughlin, 1986, p. 15).

Loss of more affluent citizens brought concomitant declines in retail trade and losses in the real estate tax base. Lost local purchasing power, coupled with the arrival of shopping malls in surrounding suburban areas, wiped out the once thriving retail district in Braddock. In just a brief period, 1972-1976, 46 businesses closed. Cultural and educational facilities were dramatically affected. A tremendous cultural asset and regional historic landmark, the Carnegie Library and Community Center of Braddock, closed in 1974. The school district was forced by court order to merge with surrounding, more affluent schools, in the early 1980s (Margolis, Burtt, and McLaughlin, 1986, p. 15).

Braddock had been one of the county's wealthiest boroughs. Yet by 1980 it was the second poorest. Rankin and North Braddock shared a similar fate, with the third and fifth lowest per capita incomes in the county (Margolis, Burtt, and McLaughlin, 1986, p. 15). In the early 1980s, as the communities of the Triborough witnessed the dramatic declines in the steel industry (and electrical production in Westinghouse facilities), they were faced with the prospect of a still dimmer future. The Edgar Thomson Works, while still functioning in Braddock and North Braddock, was working at reduced capacity with fewer workers. The only other large business in Braddock proper was Braddock Hospital. There was ample cause for fear that the mill might shut down along with others up and down the Mon Valley.

STUDY METHODS

It was within this context of decline and fear of the future that Professor Margolis and two graduate students, one from Political Science and one from the Graduate School of Public and International Affairs, undertook their study of the Triborough. Their study involved two modes of data gathering. They interviewed local leaders and surveyed individuals in area households. Specifically, students conducted telephone interviews with a representative sample of individuals (18 years of age and older) from households selected via random-digit-dialing methods. The response rate was approximately 64.3 percent, with 126 interviews completed of 196 residents selected. Interviews were also conducted, in person and over the telephone, with 35 local leaders (from government, business, labor, civic life, and religious institutions).

The research was guided by three overriding questions:

> When a long-standing community's industrial and commercial bases decline, what happens to people's attitudes toward that community? Do the people disdain the community? Do they view their hometown as unattractive or dying, a place from which to escape? (Margolis, Burtt, and McLaughlin, 1986, p. 16)

More specifically, the Triborough study focused on the perceptions of local people and leaders about their communities; their views of those communities as places to live; their concerns about contemporary problems and views on potential solutions to problems plaguing the communities; and thoughts about the future. Given the context, communities with tremendous economic difficulties, declining housing stock, poor municipal services, and lack of job opportunities, the responses of individuals were striking.

STUDY FINDINGS

The researchers reported that residents' feelings toward the communities were essentially positive. Forty-one percent viewed their community as a "good" place to live, 48 percent as "good and bad," and 11 percent as "not good." Not surprisingly, the proportions in each category varied by community, with North Braddock residents reporting more favorable feelings and Braddock residents, living in the poorest Triborough community, reporting more negative feelings. Even so, as many in Braddock viewed the community as a good place (22 percent) as viewed it as not good (Margolis, Burtt, and McLaughlin, 1986, p. 19).

Residents surveyed were able to list more things that they liked about their communities than things they disliked. Their likes, as reported by Margolis, Burtt, and McLaughlin, evidenced (and could be grouped by) strong attachments to the communities in which they lived and to positive feelings for friends and neighbors within the communities. Some few claimed to dislike their communities in general, but most dislikes were focused upon the lack of amenities and of civic, recreational, and educational institutions and services. Poor municipal services and crime rates were also viewed as problems. Fewer than 10 percent focused dislikes on particular people in strategic town positions. Most surprising, fewer than 10 percent included concerns about unemployment among their dislikes.

When asked directly about problems within the communities, however, concern about economic issues became uppermost. The researchers asked residents and local leaders to rate specific problems as important or not important. The future of the Edgar Thomson plant was viewed as important by 90 percent of the residents and 86 percent of the leadership sample. Improving housing conditions was rated important by 82 percent of both the residents and the leadership. Electing capable public officials, the future of Braddock General Hospital, maintaining strong local churches, and controlling crime were also viewed as important by a solid majority in each group. There was strong correspondence between the concerns of local residents and local leaders on the importance of community issues or problems for the Triborough: the future of the Edgar Thomson/U.S. Steel Works, the future of Braddock General Hospital, and improving housing conditions brought the endorsement of 82 to 94 percent of both leaders and residents (Margolis, Burtt, and McLaughlin, 1986, p. 21).

The study delved into several problem areas having to do with the causes of unemployment and the ways in which the situation could be improved. The results generally demonstrated that the Triborough populations were not in despair, but liked their hometowns and were willing to work to solve problems. They were concerned about the availability of resources to revitalize local industries, but they showed the inclination and the will to solve the problems. Leaders as well as residents wanted to stay in their communities. The leaders were somewhat more pessimistic about preserving and improving civic life, but both leaders and residents were attached to the Triborough and the people who lived there.

One important additional area into which the Triborough study probed was race relations. The story of Aliquippa had revealed some tensions in that respect, and community organizers found this an essential breach to try to heal in order to bring the community together for concerted action. In the Triborough, questions in the survey of residents were in simple quantitative form, and the leaders were asked to respond to more open-ended queries. On the surface, respondents gave rather bland responses indicating harmony between the races. But this picture is disrupted by a question about whether problems between blacks and whites were an important cause of the decline of Braddock's shopping district. Over half of the residents averred that racial problems were "important" (28 percent) or "somewhat important" (24 percent). In addition, a minority of respondents made comments about "blacks getting too many handouts" or "thinking the world owes them." Others expressed their feelings in an us-them terminology that indicated at least a sense of separation of the races.

The researchers felt that it was extremely important to understand this phenomenon, because, to the extent that latent racial hostility is present, it can seriously interfere with one of the great strengths of the Triborough community: "The sense of belonging and feeling of kinship with other residents is certainly weakened to some extent by the persistence of latent racism" (Margolis, Burtt, and McLaughlin, 1986, p. 30).

The team investigating and writing about the Triborough concluded its report by highlighting the paradox of the mill towns in the region in two memorable paragraphs. On the one hand, the economic and social present and future for the Triborough looked dismal:

> In many ways the face of the Triborough is extremely unattractive. Unemployment is high. The tax base is declining, the physical plant is deteriorating, the population is shrinking, and it is aging as well. Nor does there seem to be much hope of revitalization in the near future. Many ideas are under consideration, but resources are lacking. It would seem that the Triborough has all the ingredients for hopelessness and despair. (Margolis, Burtt, and McLaughlin, 1986, p. 31)

Yet, in the face of all of this uncertainty and in the midst of economic turmoil, residents were found to maintain strong attachments to the community. On the other hand, then, as is found in other mill towns, the authors describe a living entity:

> But a city is not a piece of metal. A town is not an animal. It does not "die" in a biological sense. It cannot be buried and forgotten. A section of the nation cannot be simply abandoned like a worn out tool. Our survey indicates that Braddock, North Braddock, and Rankin are still viable communities. The people who live there like their towns. They enjoy living in the Triborough, and they do not wish to migrate . . . What has happened to the Triborough is the erosion of its economic base. Jobs, and the tax revenue they generate, have disappeared. The community remains. (Margolis, Burtt, and McLaughlin, 1986, p. 32)

Chapter 7

Duquesne

The Duquesne study changed the course of studies emanating from the School of Social Work on the economic crisis. This survey was a more systematic undertaking than previous social work efforts, and did not involve the participation of students. The study was co-sponsored by the Duquesne Business Advisory Corporation. Three Social Work faculty members, James Cunningham, David Biegel, and Hide Yamatani, conducted the study. Interviews were conducted via telephone and interviewers were hired and trained by the Center for Social and Urban Research at the University of Pittsburgh. Far less time was spent in the community, although faculty met with local leaders to disseminate findings. Although the focus was still upon developing knowledge to benefit people, support program and policy decisions, and alleviate human suffering, greater effort was now being made to develop quantitative, generalizable findings to influence policymakers.

Duquesne, Pennsylvania, is a mill town situated in the Monongahela Valley near Pittsburgh. It offered the school an ideal location in which to launch its first effort at generalizable findings on the status of households in hard-hit communities. Duquesne was more representative of mill towns in the Pittsburgh region than Aliquippa, and was chosen with deliberate attention to the characteristics of mill towns. Duquesne was selected "particularly for its long time history as a major steel producing town and its relatively typical interracial population, spread of age groups, household income, educational levels, unemployment rate, and percent of workers in manufacturing" (Biegel, Cunningham, and Martz, 1986, p. 36).

*Some data from this chapter were previously presented as "Self-reliance and blue-collar unemployment in a steel town," by D. E. Biegel, J. Cunningham, H. Yamatani, and P. Martz (1989), *Social Work* 34, 399-406.

The history of Duquesne, like that of many of the mill towns in the Pittsburgh region, is focused upon the Monongahela River and its abundant natural flatlands. These flatlands are now crisscrossed with rail tracks that supplied and moved products from the mills that grew up around them. What is left of the large steel mills, which were once the focal point of Duquesne, occupies prime space on the Monongahela River.[1]

In the late 1800s, a series of corporate purchases and exchanges led to the ownership of a steel company in Duquesne by the Carnegie Steel Company. As the newly incorporated borough of Duquesne (1891) entered the twentieth century, it did so with the Carnegie Steel Company (later the Carnegie-Illinois Steel Company, U.S. Steel, and finally USX) as its sole major employer. This lack of industrial diversity was of little concern, however, for steel was doing well. The Duquesne Works was a nonunion facility in the 1800s. As labor strife rocked other steel facilities, production at full capacity continued in Duquesne.

Steelmaking in Duquesne, as in other communities, was linked to wartime efforts. Following World War I, demand for production lessened somewhat, but steelmaking continued in the locality. Duquesne celebrated its Golden Jubilee in 1941 as World War II called for increased steel production. In Duquesne and in the neighboring mill town of Homestead, the government was involved in a massive effort to expand steel production for the war. In Homestead, a large neighborhood was razed and approximately 10,000 residents were relocated. In Duquesne, something similar occurred but the number of people involved was smaller. For outsiders, such a large-scale displacement of people might be expected to be accompanied by unparalleled unrest. Not everyone welcomed these moves; however, the marriage of war to steel gave birth to prosperity and the relationship was viewed positively by many.

> Before the year [1941] is out the closely-packed dwellings of its more than 2700 inhabitants will be leveled to the ground, and in their place will rise a huge new addition to the Duquesne Steel Works . . . Thus is sacrificed to the march of industry the part of Duquesne longest associated with the city's history. But there will be few tears shed when the people of Duquesne

watch its demolition. For they know that its passing means more Duquesne-made steel–and in Duquesne, more steel means more money in the bank and more food on the table. (Ball, 1941)

Interestingly, steel producers recognized that excess production would be the inevitable consequence of such expansion, and at first they balked at the government's initial efforts to induce this. Following World War II, adjustments in work schedules were made, and Duquesne and other mill towns started down the path of slow decline.

The birth of suburbs led to the out-migration of residents. In 1930 the City of Duquesne had a population of 21,396. Fifty years later, in 1980, the city's population was cut in half, to 10,094. Many of these "movers" stayed close to home, shifting to the more spacious homes of West Mifflin abutting Duquesne. They created a natural community of Duquesne that encompassed more than just the city's borders.

In 1980 the unemployment rate for Duquesne was 8.9 percent, far from rosy. The plant shutdowns of the 1980s were catastrophic to Duquesne, however, altering with speed the experiences of generations. In Duquesne, as in Aliquippa, gradual decline experienced over decades gave way to sudden, almost complete economic chaos. The suddenness of this change was critical to the School of Social Work's interest in such communities and to its efforts to develop meaningful findings about the links between economic crisis and the experiences of individual households and communities.

STUDY METHODS

Building upon the preliminary explorations of Aliquippa, the Duquesne household survey sought to answer the following questions:

1. How extensive are unemployment and underemployment, change in income, and other economic impacts among the town's households, five years after the beginning of the economic recession of the 1980s?
2. What measures have households taken to maintain and/or restore their economic position?

3. What role have social agencies and other community institutions played in the efforts of households to recover?
4. How do mill town households view the future?
5. What major issues need to be addressed to improve a mill town's chances for recovery? (Biegel, Cunningham, and Martz, 1986)

The sample of Duquesne households was developed by selecting every fifth name from street lists of residents with connected telephones contained in the Cole Directory for Allegheny County. Streets included in the sampling frame were all of those in the City of Duquesne and adjoining streets in West Mifflin.[2] In this manner, 805 households were selected; 401 completed household surveys (50 percent) resulted. The refusal rate was 40 percent (282 households); 12 percent (95) could not be reached or were nonresidential and 4 percent (27) participated only partially.

The questionnaire used was made up of 38 items related to: employment status; economic and social conditions; responses to unemployment; attitudes toward and relations with organizations promoting employment or providing services; and the future expectations of households. The interviews were structured to take approximately 15 minutes on the telephone.

THE SAMPLE

The respondents in the Duquesne study were representative of the area in terms of gender and household size. However, black households were underrepresented. The significant decline in workers in manufacturing was expected, as was the increased average age, and as was increased unemployment. It was assumed that many younger people would have left the area during 1979 and 1980, and that unemployment would have increased dramatically (Biegel, Cunningham, and Martz, 1986). The entire sample of 401 households contained 1,009 household members. The average household comprised 2.5 people. Almost two-thirds of the households (65 percent) were nuclear families and 36 (9 percent) were extended families and eight (2 percent) were unrelated groups.

STUDY FINDINGS

The respondents in these households provided the school with dramatic data. Five years after the recession of the early 1980s, and two years after the first forays into Aliquippa, unemployment rates were still at double-digit levels. Forty-six percent of all households with one or more members in the labor force in 1986 (hereafter called a labor force household) had at least one member laid off in the prior five years. Thirty-eight percent of all 1986 labor force members were laid off in the five years prior to the study. One-third (33 percent) of labor force households had a household member laid off one year or more and 24 percent of these households had a household member laid off more than once (Biegel, Cunningham, and Martz, 1986; Biegel, Cunningham, Yamatani, and Martz, 1989).

It should be noted that these unemployment rates included "all who want work and don't have it," which is not how official U.S. unemployment rates are calculated (Biegel, Cunningham, and Martz, 1986, p. 47). The double-digit figures were confirmed, however, by an independent survey done by journalists in which graduating high school students were asked about their fathers' current work status: 21 percent reported that their fathers were unemployed and 13 percent stated that they were working only part-time (Blotzer, 1986). Limited data from black households in the Duquesne survey indicated that the employment situation for minorities was far worse, with 50 percent of black households having at least one unemployed member.

Income levels provided further confirmation that the community had fallen upon hard times. Fifty-four percent of those working were earning less than $7.00 per hour. Median annual household incomes were less than $16,000 (even if all of the 13 percent who did not provide incomes were over $16,000). The authors of the first report on the survey noted that, between 1980 and 1986, the consumer price index had increased 39 percent. To sustain comparable purchasing power, the median income of Duquesne households in 1980 ($14,613) would have needed to be increased to $20,312 (Biegel, Cunningham, and Martz, 1986, p. 50). Nearly three-fifths (57 percent) of the households in the sample reported incomes less than $16,001. A third of the households reported incomes of less than

$10,001, with 18 percent of these with less than $7,001. At the higher end of the income scale, 2 percent reported incomes of $50,001 or more. Eight percent had incomes between $30,001 and $50,000.

Sixty-nine percent of those interviewed reported having been affected by unemployment, 39 percent of these "a lot" and 30 percent of these "a little." Twenty-nine percent reported that they had not been affected at all. When asked to assess their overall economic situation, 22 percent of those interviewed viewed it as poor or very poor and 44 percent saw their situation as fair. However, one-third (33 percent) viewed their overall situation as good or very good.

Their views of their personal household situations stand in some contrast to their views of the overall community. Eighty percent of those interviewed saw Duquesne's economic condition as poor or very poor. Only 5 percent viewed economic conditions as good or very good for the community. As noted on several occasions earlier, a theme of interest across the community studies was how people, particularly those directly affected by unemployment, were surviving in the wake of large-scale plant closings. The results that emerged from the Duquesne survey confirmed much of the indirect data students gathered in the earliest and later observations of Aliquippa. People were not sitting idly by as the crisis struck (Biegel, Cunningham, and Martz, 1986).

While the following does not represent mutually exclusive household member activity (some of the households sampled may have had members engaged in more than one of the following activities), 60 households (15 percent) reported that a member had moved out to seek work, 30 households (7.5 percent) had a member who had tried to start a new business, and 67 (17 percent) had a member seeking an education. Only 21 (5 percent) had a member seeking retraining. The authors of the study noted that local leaders believed that the small number of people seeking retraining was due either to a tradition of pride and self-reliance or a lack of faith in retraining as a means to a job.

Just over half of those who left the area to seek work elsewhere (52 percent of 67 people from 60 households) were under 25 years of age and all save one had at least a high school education. Thirty-one percent were between the ages of 25 and 30 and 17 percent were over 30 years of age (with the oldest being 47). Seventy-two percent of those leaving went to another state and approximately 78 percent of them were still working out of state at the time of the survey. The young who left thus appeared to be finding opportunities. The findings confirmed the wisdom of the advice being given to youth in the Electric Valley by local leaders and the advice those interviewed in Duquesne said that they would offer young people. Forty-seven percent of those interviewed in Duquesne would advise children to get an education and 32 percent would advise them to move from the area. Fifteen households reported that friends or relatives had moved in due to unemployment, doubling up as a survival strategy. A little over half of these (eight) viewed this as a problem and seven did not.

While households were making efforts to recover in resourceful ways, making use of formal services and organizations was not a favored help-seeking activity. The researchers involved in the Duquesne survey were struck by the findings. While 46 percent of the households had been directly affected by layoffs, fewer than one in five households (17 percent) tried to get help from "an agency, church, institution, nationality group, or other organization during the past five years" (Biegel, Cunningham, and Martz, 1986). Only 3.5 percent (14) reported that they needed counseling assistance; 24 percent reported needing help to find a job, and 23 percent needed education. Fewer than 7 percent reported needing rent assistance or food and only 1.5 percent reported needing help for their mortgage.

In terms of seeking and obtaining help for the needs that they had, households more frequently sought and obtained help for medical needs. Help finding a job was reported as a need by the largest percentage of the sample (24 percent), yet it was the help least often obtained (for those who actually sought assistance). Of note, the low numbers of families reporting active help-seeking from formal agencies and organizations is not a completely accurate picture of the extent of help provided by the formal sector, since some income transfer policies were involved.

In the wake of a massive plant closing, the question had to be asked: what are the sources of income people are depending upon? The social insurances (social security, unemployment insurance, and workers' compensation) and income support programs (for example, general public assistance) figured prominently in the support of households, as did private pensions. Forty-eight percent of the households had someone receiving a social security check. Thirty percent of the households had someone receiving a pension check. Unemployment compensation was benefiting someone in 10 percent of the households. Eight percent of the households had a member benefiting from public assistance with 11 percent of the households having someone benefiting from food stamps. The percentages of households with members receiving public assistance seemed low considering the income levels of the households previously discussed. The authors of the original report were unsure of the extent to which pride and self-reliance were keeping households from seeking such help or the extent to which households may have underreported cash assistance received and its sources.

The apparent lack of active help-seeking from the formal sector in many areas was viewed as troubling to the authors of the original report because many of those households that did seek help were quite successful in obtaining it, particularly in meeting health care needs. Interestingly, the lack of help-seeking behavior on the part of households did not correspond to their willingness to give help to others. When respondents were asked about their involvement in organizations to help the unemployed, 50 (12.5 percent) reported that they were involved at the time of the study, donating an average of 17 hours of volunteer time per month. When asked about their willingness to join or help an organization to aid the unemployed, 32 percent said that they would probably join or offer assistance; 37 percent said that they would have to say no; and 28 percent were not sure.

The authors of the study concluded that the traditional, ethnic, self-reliant nature of the households of the community continued to hold sway in the face of extreme economic conditions. Duquesne had clearly been hard hit by the shutdown of the massive U.S. Steel plant at the heart of Duquesne. Approximately one-fifth of the workers in the households surveyed were unemployed at the time of the study. An additional 8 percent were underemployed, desiring full-time work but able to find only part-time work. Thirty-eight percent had been laid off in the past five years. Twenty-six percent had experienced a layoff lasting a year or more, and 19 percent had experienced more than one layoff in the prior five years.

Still, they remained remarkably optimistic about the future of their own households. In the year ahead, a third (33 percent) saw their future being a little better and 10 percent thought it would be much better. Five years ahead, 25 percent thought their households would be a little better off and 25 percent thought they would be much better off. They stated this even as they provided a less rosy view of the employment situation in the Pittsburgh area for the same period. Just over half (52 percent) viewed the employment situation as being the same or worse in the next five years; only 38 percent thought it would be better.

The authors of the report on Duquesne concluded:

> What comes out of the data is a hope springs eternal view of the future for many households in the community hedged by realistic, less sanguine, advice for their children. The past has happy endings, and likely the present crisis, too, will pass away as crises always have within living memory—but just in case it doesn't, let's get our kids educated and off to a job-plenty area . . . (Biegel, Cunningham, and Martz, 1986, p. 66)

IN SUMMARY

At the close of the study, those involved in the River Communities Project reexamined the data from the five community studies—the two Aliquippa studies, the Electric Valley study, the Triborough study, and the Duquesne survey. What was known now and what questions were emerging for further study?

What was known now was that the extent of damage to entire communities was significant. Local government revenues were falling dramatically, unemployment rates in individual communities and neighborhoods were at Depression-era levels, and the gradual decline in population experienced in the area for decades began to look like an exodus. As bleak as things appeared, people persevered and the communities continued, smaller, poorer, economically devastated, but hopeful.

Several areas presented themselves both for further study and as opportunities to develop programs and policies. If these communities were to have futures, some able youth would need to either stay behind or move in. Those involved in the project became interested in creating opportunities for youth and in improving the education offered to them to better prepare them for the future. Disparities of income and job opportunities along racial lines seemed apparent in Aliquippa and in the limited data on black families in the Duquesne survey. Latent discrimination was evidenced in the Triborough. The project thus also became interested in learning more about the differential impact of the crisis upon black households. Strategies to bring about a better future would have to involve and improve the lot of the oldest and the youngest, the most vulnerable, the poorest, the most discriminated against, and the least skilled—those frequently trapped in devastated communities.

NOTES

1. As this is being written (1994) the Duquesne Works is being rapidly dismantled. Most of what was once the Homestead Works of U.S. Steel has already been taken down and scrapped. Miles of riverfront property remain bare and undeveloped.

2. Community leaders had identified streets in census tracts 4882 and 4884 as a spillover area considered part of the greater Duquesne community traditionally. These streets were included for this reason. These streets were described as those with ". . . newer homes to which steel and other industrial workers migrated during the prosperous period, from 1945 through 1970. It was a way that families could move up to suburban housing without really leaving their old community." (Biegel, Cunningham, and Martz, 1986).

PART FOUR:
TRAGEDY AND HUMAN RESPONSE

To a large extent, the exploratory results determined the future of the River Communities Project. The findings responded to the two questions posed for the first project phase. Local statistics that showed some evidence of economic revival in the Pittsburgh area did not apply to the mill towns. Aliquippa was not the sole victim of economic collapse; a whole area was affected. The distress was widespread, and it was not only enduring but also deepening as time passed. Years after the crisis of the early 1980s, there was no evidence of improvement in the life circumstances of the residents of the mill towns or in the condition of their communities. On the contrary, the towns were perceived as becoming steadily worse off with lessening hope for renewal.

The job situation remained dismal. Advice to children living in the area was reported overwhelmingly to be "Get the best education you can, and GET OUT!" In Braddock, arguably the most devastated community in the region, researchers reported that the economy was dead, although the community lived on. Other declining mill towns appeared to be headed in the same direction. Yet that phrase about the community's living on was a recurring theme in the research reports from the first phase. Large majorities of the community leaders interviewed stated that they felt that many residents saw their towns as their homes and wanted to stay there. The leaders themselves were willing to work with an overall development group controlled by local people in hopes of revitalizing their towns. Although the population of the communities continued to shrink, and the infrastructures and services continued to diminish, there was evidence of loyalty to place in spite of all the problems.

Results also indicated that families were helping members to survive, and that churches and ethnic associations were contributing to the survival of residents. Some local institutions were trying to respond to the need for job creation efforts. There was commitment on the part of many leaders and residents, but there was also fear and alienation due to increasing crime rates and fewer police available. Racial tension grows with continuing job scarcity. The communities have become more and more divided against themselves as the downhill slide continues. What can be done to help these communities?

The overall purpose of the River Communities Project was to gain a more comprehensive understanding of the large-scale job dislocation in the region and to contribute to the development of policies, programs, and services to effectively address the social consequences of severe and enduring economic distress. The first phase of the project was launched very rapidly after results of the first Aliquippa study provided evidence of continuing suffering in at least one mill town. The executive committee was very pleased to be able to secure a small launching grant, but much of the research depended on volunteer efforts by faculty and by students in Social Work and, in one study, in the Political Science department in cooperation with the Graduate School of Public and International Affairs. Concern over the fate of the neighboring communities and an interest in action-oriented research motivated faculty. To accomplish the work as quickly as feasible under the circumstances, faculty trained graduate students and gave them firsthand supervised experience in the field.

Whole classes sometimes pitched in, not only to collect the data, but also to learn how to do coding and data analysis. Students were usually rewarded with class credit for their efforts and, in some cases at least, there was added delight when this credit was applied to a novel approach to what was often perceived as a dull, dry, and difficult curriculum requirement: research methods. Faculty and students also worked in teams to put the findings together and write up individual project reports. Other faculty and students joined in to do editing and polishing. Clerical staff, too, contributed greatly to the speed with which study results were made available. Phase I only began early in 1986, yet by the late summer of 1986, four studies had been produced and disseminated in three bound reports.

The alacrity that pervaded the cooperative process allowed the ten-member executive committee described earlier to move to the second phase of the project. That the Dean had constituted this able group early in the preliminary stage, so that the members were ready to work intensively when called upon, also helped enormously to make it possible to immediately make use of the reports to develop a formal proposal for funding for the second phase. The scattered small research projects of the first phase did the necessary exploratory work, but a more unified, overall research plan was needed for the second phase. The project now needed more carefully designed and integrated efforts to fulfill goals. And while voluntary contributions on the part of the faculty would still continue to play a large role in carrying out the studies, formal and systematic research procedures would require more extensive financial support. Thus a proposal titled *The River Communities Research and Demonstration Project: Phase II* was prepared for submission to potential funding sources.

For the second phase of the project, more specific major objectives were articulated. The emphasis was on research that would focus in on the households of mill towns with more depth and precision and consolidate evidence of particular household constellations and their needs and capacities. Dissemination of the findings could then be used to develop self-help projects by the communities with school assistance.

Three objectives were outlined:

1. To conduct a longitudinal survey of 1,200 households in six river communities to increase our understanding of the effects of unemployment and economic dislocation over time, and to better assist local policymakers.
2. To coordinate the development of several individual research projects investigating the impact of economic transition on specific population groups.
3. To plan and initiate regional miniconferences of community leaders and residents in river communities to review research findings and develop policy initiatives and plans for demonstration projects. *(The River Communities Research and Demonstration Project: Phase II,* pp. 12-13.)

Action research would continue to be a very large part of the second-phase activities. There was some research available on individual plant closings and their consequences, but nothing was found on the level of a regional disaster such as the one that occurred in southwestern Pennsylvania. Had the case study focused on a more limited damaged space, it might have been possible to move more rapidly into an extensive community organization and demonstration phase. In the river communities, however, it seemed crucial to learn more about the impact of this widespread catastrophe before encouraging more than modest efforts.

In order to procure the very best research products available, the executive committee developed an overall research plan for the River Communities Project. The plan endorsed expanding participation to include faculty from other disciplines and departments throughout the University. Each study proposal submitted for consideration in the second phase was subject to peer review evaluation of the efficacy of its design in relation to the goals of the project. To improve the process of proposal writing, selection, and implementation, two graduate students were recruited to work on the project, one as a full-time coordinator and the other as a part-time research associate.

From the total submitted, eight proposals were judged to fulfill the criteria set for acceptability. One was for the first wave of the longitudinal survey. Phase one had already demonstrated that measures repeated over time would be important to assess changes in the economic state of the region, since the economic downturn was proving to be of long duration. This study received funding from a local foundation for the first wave to consist of a random telephone survey of six communities considered to be overall a good collective yardstick of the river communities. The plan was to carry out the longitudinal study every year to gauge the progress or lack thereof of the mill towns for the near future. In fact, funding was obtained for just three surveys before the end of the project: one in 1988, one in 1991, and one in 1993. In Chapter 8, findings from the first survey are presented. In the last part of this book, it will be possible to look again at the fate of the mill towns in the findings in 1993, some ten years after the preliminary research was carried out in Aliquippa.

Four other studies were carried out from the remaining seven. In three cases local foundations provided support. A final small project was funded by a grant from the University of Pittsburgh. The two foundations that supported the research had limited monies to spend and they chose those pieces that experience in the community suggested dealt with especially vulnerable roles and family configurations. In-depth research would sharpen the focus on those factors across and within particular types of households that would provide targets for intervention and be linked to policy considerations.

The first selection demonstrated a concern with women in households where unemployment had occurred. It was suggested that families may pile additional burdens on women when the chief breadwinner loses his job or when women themselves become unemployed chief breadwinners. Second, a project was selected that focused on the elderly, who might be either left behind when younger family members moved away to seek a more promising job market or called upon to share meager resources with unemployed adult children. A third project chosen centered on fatherhood and unemployment. Data suggested that unemployed fathers, inexperienced in caretaking responsibilities, might have problems when called upon to take care of their young children if their wives went out of the home to support the family. Directly or indirectly, themes in the exploratory material all reverberated around young people, and an additional small study was carried out with small-grant University funding to add more information about youth in areas of high unemployment. The first longitudinal survey results and the findings from research on these other four themes are presented in Part Four. The very last pages of Part Four summarize the results. Because the data so far indicated that black individuals and families were suffering disproportionately, all projects were designed to include subsamples of participants who were African American.

A methodological note is useful before going on to present the five studies in the chapters of Part Four and their results. First, because researchers were given some autonomy in developing their designs, choosing their samples, and constructing instruments, and because full-time faculty members who conducted the research had limited opportunities for close collaboration, the studies varied in content perhaps more than was strictly desirable. All studies included data on the impact of the disaster in terms of employment, income, and other material consequences. All also included themes around informal and formal network assistance and support. However, each study varied somewhat from the others in the emphasis given to particular themes. The data are not therefore strictly comparable from study to study. There is, it will be seen, nevertheless a good measure of comparability combined with a unique flavor for each separate piece.

Second, there was discrepancy in measurement approaches to symptoms of depression. In all studies except the one on the elderly, clinical depression was a concern for individuals whose lives had been subject to catastrophic stress. Two studies, the one on women with unemployment in their households and the one on unemployed fathers, used a validated depression scale. The studies on the six communities and on youth asked simple standardized questions on whether the respondent had had a problem with depression, anxiety, or nervousness during the past three years and relied on the perceptions of the respondents. Across the studies, it will be seen that the evidence for depression is relatively low, although there are some interesting differences between subgroups, especially in the six-town survey. The highest levels, which were still modest, were found among single mothers in the survey and mothers in the unemployed fathers research.

The proposal for the second phase of the River Communities Project was sent to potential funding sources in the context of the total project, which was to consist of three phases. The third phase was intended to put the results into action through projects of various kinds to help communities. One widespread community need was very clear from the exploratory phase and that was for community organization. The mill towns showed a high level of divisiveness in the face of the terrible devastation the residents were suffering. The project agreed to assist communities in mounting projects, and a number of community organization and demonstration projects were brought into being as a consequence of the action research findings. Although not intended to blossom quite so soon, one community organization project was inspired by the first study in Aliquippa. The project started when a master's student who lived in Aliquippa did a community organization field placement there. It became an expansive and versatile effort over the years, and is used as a star example of what can be accomplished and what is beyond reach without substantial outside help in a region as devastated as the one being studied. The story of Aliquippa and several other community organization projects is told in Part Five, as well as the developments and outcomes in a series of Youth Enterprise Demonstration Projects. Faculty from the school were able to find ways of helping in a fairly large number of community efforts in a relatively short time, and only those that were the most carefully documented are included in this book.

Chapter 8

Battered Households

Hide Yamatani
Lambert Maguire
Robin K. Rogers
Mary Lou O'Kennedy

. . . just last week, Jimmy learned that his bank had begun proceedings to foreclose his mortgage, that his truck had been repossessed, and that his medical coverage was in jeopardy. As if that weren't enough, he wound up in intensive care for a diabetes-related problem.

David Corn
"The Mon Valley Mourns for Steel"
Harper's, September, 1996

Declining household economies are readily understood as indicators of serious problems for families and communities. During the 1980s and continuing today, safety nets for dislocated workers and the new working poor were being eliminated or cut back even as joblessness mounted. In the wake of back-to-back recessions and double-digit unemployment in the river communities, it became important to look at the conditions of households periodically to assess the continuing impact of industrial collapse and gauge the future for families and communities. Thus, in 1988, the first of a series of inquiries into area households was begun (Yamatani, Maguire, Rogers, and O'Kennedy, 1989). Although, at that time, broad economic indicators for both the nation and southwestern Pennsylvania suggested that economic recovery was on the way, data from small community studies strongly indicated continued depression in the mill towns.

Accordingly, to learn about family conditions across the area, 1,211 heads of household were interviewed by phone in six communities. Approximately 200 interviews were conducted with heads of households in each of the six communities. The attained response rates ranged from 60 to 64 percent in these communities. The households were selected via random-digit dialing. Four of the six communities were a mix of traditional mill towns: Aliquippa, Clairton, McKeesport, and Monessen. To augment the sample with some regional diversity, Brownsville, an older community once but no longer prosperous through the coal trade, and Washington, a community adjacent to the declining river valleys with a more diverse economic base, were added. In each of the communities, the households were selected by random-digit telephone dialing, a method selected and carried out with the cooperation of the University Center for Social and Urban Research. Sixty percent of those called and reached participated in interviews.

The household study was undertaken to provide specific information in five primary areas: economic status, employment, education, physical and mental health, and crime. These areas were selected for attention because they have been highlighted in the abundant literature on unemployment and its effects. As in the other studies reported on in this chapter, special attention will be paid to the most vulnerable population groups.

Unemployment in the 1980s was "real" in the sense that it was unavoidable and placed Pittsburgh and much of the rest of the nation in a situation for which no ameliorative policy exists (Murray, 1984). Workers had every reason to expect the loss of jobs and income, yet social programs were being cut back at the time. It could be expected that white, well-educated males would fare relatively well, while blacks and women, especially female single heads of households, would be the most damaged (Sidel, 1986). Beyond loss of income, and possibly sinking into poverty, unemployment has been found to have other devastating effects, especially on physical and mental health. Brenner (1973) used a historical analytic framework to correlate varied health and mental health data with economic trends in this country between 1950 and 1980. He used a number of indicators of social stress, such as total mortality rates, cirrhosis of the liver, mental hospital admissions, and total suicides, and found the rates to rise significantly in the wake of recessions. Employing a different methodology, Gore (1978) examined a wide spectrum of physical- and mental-health-related problems in a population of men before their jobs were terminated and at several intervals thereafter. She was especially interested in the degree to which social supports could intervene to lessen the impact of economic deprivation. Gore found that unemployed men who had low social supports were particularly adversely affected by the loss of their jobs compared to those whose social supports were higher. These were some of the leads followed by the researchers in collecting and analyzing the survey data.

EMPLOYMENT, UNEMPLOYMENT, AND TRAINING

The impact of unemployment was acute, pervasive, and persistent in the traditional industrial communities along the rivers in the Pittsburgh area. The survey was carried out several years after the worst of the economic storm had hit, and it confirmed that the river communities suffered long-lasting devastation. In early 1988, the survey data showed that the unadjusted average unemployment rate, that is, "a head of household desiring employment who cannot find employment," was 23.5 percent. Across the six communities surveyed, only 42 percent of the household heads were employed. Even in Washington, which had a more diversified and robust economy than the other five communities, only 50.2 percent were working. Among those working, it was found that they had been unemployed an average of 2.5 months during the previous three years. If one looks only at those who have suffered any unemployment at all, however, the average length of unemployment jumps to 12.1 months, more than a full year out of the three. For those unemployed at the time of the interview, the picture was even more bleak. For the same three-year period, these household heads had been unemployed an average of 21.5 months, or almost two years. Even a higher level of education correlated only weakly with a higher level of employment, partly because the distribution of employment by occupational classification had changed in the region. A shift had occurred in which over 100,000 of the better-paying industrial jobs were lost, while 40,000 lower-paying nonmanufacturing jobs were gained.

The nonworking heads of households in this sample who wanted to work very definitely did not share the characteristics of the long-term unemployed: only 6 percent of them were on welfare or were high school dropouts. These household heads longed for work, and they avoided welfare even though close to half had incomes below the government standard for the poverty level for their family size. Income was low, however, even for those who were employed. Being employed, for example, did not save 8.6 percent of the households with working heads from poverty-level incomes. Unlike employment, education was a good predictor of household income. The higher the level of education, the higher the income was likely to be.

Many people in the six communities were "displaced workers," that is, they were struggling to adjust when their once valued skills became obsolete. Not only those who formerly held high-paying manufacturing jobs, but also those just entering the workplace and those still in school, needed to struggle to find a way to manage in a changing work world. One possibility was through access to job preparation programs and retraining in the six communities, for training is seen as the key to survival in a rapidly changing job market. Questions were therefore asked about those who wanted job training in this sample and those who received it. Contrary to the myths about steelworkers being unwilling to try something new at a lower wage, dropouts to whom the future means nothing, and single women with kids happy to stay at home and collect welfare, almost one-third (30 percent) of the household heads in this sample expressed a desire for training. Moreover, those who would have been considered the least likely candidates expressed the most interest. Overall, one in five respondents (20 percent) received some job training during the three years preceding the survey. Unfortunately, however, among those who desired training, the ones with the greatest need because they were high school dropouts were the least likely to receive training (1.8 percent), high school graduates were more likely to receive training (12.9 percent), and those with education beyond high school were the most likely of all to receive training (23.3 percent). Did the training lead to positive results? According to the data, close to two-thirds of the respondents (65.6 percent) who received training reported benefiting because it prepared them to get or keep a job, to find a better job, or to obtain a promotion. Only 10.4 percent indicated that training was "no help at all," and the small remainder said it was too early to assess the results. This all sounds like a great success, until a comparison is made between those who were already employed when they received training, and those who were unemployed at that time. The results show that 75 percent of the positive outcomes were for those who were employed and only 25 percent were for the unemployed. The most dismaying finding is that 60 percent of the respondents who received job training were unemployed at the time of the interview.

For two populations found to be most vulnerable in the dismal job market, blacks and single female heads of households, the damage inflicted by massive unemployment was far worse. Blacks on the average were approximately three times more often jobless (32.6 percent) than their white counterparts (10.6 percent). Single female heads of households of either race were similarly affected, suffering three times more unemployment (31.3 percent) compared to married heads of households (10.7 percent). The situation for blacks and for single female heads of households was exacerbated by inequities in the world of work even when they held jobs. Although blacks held a slight advantage in managerial and professional specialty jobs (16.3 percent) compared with whites (13.4 percent), blacks were far more likely to be employed in service occupations (42.8 percent) than whites (28 percent), who held the better-paying jobs in precision production, in craft and repair work, or as operators and fabricators. Single female heads of households were also heavily concentrated in service jobs (37.5 percent), far outnumbering even their single male counterparts (28 percent).

White households had significantly more income than black households, whether the head was employed, unemployed, or retired. Marital status also was related to income as well as gender, and female-headed households were on the bottom rung of the ladder. The wage segregation suffered by blacks and single females, and the heightened incidence of unemployment, left incredible numbers in poverty. Over half (52.2 percent) of the unemployed blacks in the sample were living below the poverty level at the time of the survey. For single unemployed females the situation was even worse, with three out of five households (60 percent) below the poverty level. Although the findings show that blacks and single females were extremely vulnerable to economic hardship and the most desirous of job training, they were least likely to receive it. Thirty-four percent of black heads of households and 25 percent of single female heads of household desired training but did not get training. If employed, these two groups were clustered in low-paying jobs with little possibility of advancement. All groups in the sample endured hardship, but these two most vulnerable groups were forced into living at the margins of society in the stricken mill towns.

SOCIAL COSTS AND SOCIAL SUPPORTS

Unemployment and poverty can also rob people of their physical and mental health and general well-being. Given the dramatic job losses and severe stresses associated with the shutdown of Pittsburgh's steel industry, the researchers anticipated that sample members would have many problems. The goal for this part of the survey was to establish the differential impact of stress on specific populations. Recognizing that the elderly are considered to be a "population at risk" in health areas, the total sample was divided first into three age groups. For serious physical illnesses such as heart disease, diabetes, and cancer, those 65 or older did have significantly higher rates (43.8 percent) than those 41 to 64 (30 percent) and those 40 or younger (22.7 percent) among the heads of households. But when mental-health-related variables such as depression and serious family arguments were considered, the linear relationship by age disappeared. The youngest among the sample population had the highest depression rates (16.6 percent), followed by the oldest group (11.9 percent), with the middle group lowest (11.2 percent). Only a very small proportion (4.2 percent) of the sample reported serious family arguments, although again the youngest group had the highest rates (8.6 percent).

Employment status is a more powerful influence than age in some areas, although physical health rates remained more related to age. Again other variables that have been used before, race, gender, and marital status, are related to emotional well-being. The unemployed heads of households had a 25.2 percent rate of depression compared with a 10.9 percent rate for the employed. Married heads of household had lower rates of depression (11.8 percent) than single female heads of household (21.3 percent), but single male heads of households had the lowest rates of all (9.2 percent). Since the single males had higher income levels and fewer dependents, the difference between them and the single females is understandable. Perhaps, in such terrible times, it was a relief to some single men not to even have a spouse.

Many people interviewed for this study were suffering from physical and mental health problems. Where did they go for help and how satisfied were they with the help received? Survey results show that the sources of help were split between informal service networks or support systems such as relatives and friends and the formal service system composed of doctors, social workers, and other trained professionals. Well over two-fifths of the sample (45.3 percent) said they never sought help from anyone. Those who did seek help were about evenly divided between going to the informal or the formal system.

The level of satisfaction with help obtained varied between the two systems. Respondents were generally more satisfied with help given by informal network persons; three-quarters (75 percent) were either very satisfied or satisfied with help from relatives and nine-tenths (90 percent) with help from friends or neighbors. Satisfaction was high in the formal sector as well, with almost two-thirds (66.6 percent) who went to doctors and just over two-thirds (70.6 percent) who asked for help from mental health centers being very satisfied or satisfied.

However, unlike with the informal system of relatives and friends, a sizable proportion were very dissatisfied with formal care. Over one-quarter (26.7 percent) were very dissatisfied with their doctors and a slightly larger proportion (29.4 percent) were very dissatisfied with care received from mental health centers. It may well be that more severe problems, physical and mental, are brought to formal service providers, while at the same time the expectations are higher. Overall, however, the respondents did report attention to their health needs when they asked for help, and certainly most were satisfied with help received. Support systems in the six communities, informal and formal, seemed to have been functioning quite well.

OTHER SOCIAL COSTS, OTHER PROBLEMS

Beyond the effects on individuals, the costs to communities of the recession of the 1980s, combined with cuts in service programs, had serious consequences for the small municipalities up and down the river valleys of the Pittsburgh region. With rising unemployment and underemployment, the municipalities lost most of their tax base. While they often tried all kinds of measures for cost cutting or revenue saving, the level of desperation eventually led to the laying off of firefighters, ambulance service workers, and police. Small bankrupt mill towns had little access to state and federal dollars to ameliorate their distress. One of the consequences was rising fear, as reported by the respondents, especially fear of crime. The respondents were in most cases long-term residents of their communities, and many reported increasing crime rates in their neighborhoods. Households with an unemployed head suffered the highest rates of criminal victimization, and their lack of trust in what was left of the local police was evident. Unemployed households were the most likely to take their own protective measures, such as purchasing guns or weapons and improving access to weapons. Employed household heads who believed that the crime rate was increasing were also more likely to take preventive measures.

Massive unemployment in the six communities added to the multiple stresses associated with job loss and poverty the sense of not having safety in one's own home in a neighborhood where once everyone seemed to know everyone else. Again it is the unemployed who bear the brunt of victimization and fear of victimization.

IN SUMMARY

This random survey of 1,211 heads of households found double-digit unemployment still strangling families more than five years after the collapse of manufacturing. Blacks and single females were unemployed at much higher rates than whites and single males.

Those unemployed for longer periods were less likely to find jobs, and again blacks and single females among the heads of households were disproportionately likely to be long-term unemployed. When employed, these two groups were in lower-paying positions.

As a result, whites, whether employed, unemployed, or retired, had higher incomes than blacks. Single female heads of households had the lowest income levels of all. As reported in the text, over half the blacks and three-fifths of the single females who were unemployed were living below the poverty level for their household size. White respondents were far less likely to be below the poverty level, but even among employed whites 8.4 percent were below the poverty line. Education was consistently associated with earnings, that is, those with higher educational levels had higher incomes. But it was less a factor in length of time unemployed, especially for blacks, for whom level of education made no difference at all.

Far from sitting back and hoping the mills would just reopen and require their labor, the heads of households showed great interest in training and education. Training and educational opportunities, however, fell very disproportionately to those already employed. And the rate of unemployment among those who had received training or education was very disappointing. Worse still, those who needed training most were the least likely to get it even when they desired it: the blacks, the single females, and the high school dropouts.

At the time of the survey, not surprisingly, many respondents were having difficulties with physical and mental health. Older, retired respondents were having, predictably, more problems with physical health. Unemployed respondents were having more mental-health-related problems with depression and serious family arguments. Single female heads reported the highest level of depression of all, which was not surprising given their low income and relatively high level of dependents. One bright spot here is that those who asked for help for their problems were usually satisfied with what they received.

It is sad to note that the widespread suffering among the working people of southwestern Pennsylvania was further increased by the sense of no longer being safe in their homes as the ability of the mill towns to provide police services was diminished. Unfortunately, the residents of this area are subjected to many kinds of suffering.

Chapter 9

When Unemployment Strikes: The Responses of Women in Households

Martha Baum
Barbara K. Shore
Kathy Fleissner

All of my dreams have been washed away.

Study Respondent

The findings from the battered households study demonstrated the plight of the mill towns on a broad level. The area had evidently experienced no meaningful recovery five to six years after economic disaster struck. The special focus in this study was on women in households where unemployment had occurred. A major concern was with the multiple roles women play in households and how these change and with what effects in times of financial crisis (Baum, Shore, and Fleissner, 1988).

The research was exploratory since this was a relatively untapped area in existing studies. In-depth, face-to-face interviews were conducted because there were a large number of questions, many of which were open-ended. The sample consisted of 152 women. Initial lists of potential respondents were obtained from telephone surveys in two river communities that had been hard hit by regional economic downturn. The sample was purposive. Only women who,

Some data from this chapter were previously published as "Women and economic crisis: The untold story," *Affilia* 8(1): 9-25. Baum, M., Shore, B. K., and Fleissner, K. (1993).

in a telephone contact, were found to be living in a household with at least one other family member and where at least one household member had experienced unemployment in the last six years were invited to be interviewed. To ensure variety, half of the women were 20 to 40 years of age and the other half over 40 to 60. In conformity with regional distribution by race, about a quarter of the respondents were black (27.5 percent) and the remainder white. Marital status and household size also varied among the final sample, although respondents were not specifically chosen to reflect such variation.

Little attention has been paid to women except as assistant bread-winners in times of economic crisis, although the literature does show that women are the family members most likely to manage stress in troubled families (Kranichfield, 1987). Renewed interest in the impact of stress on family life (Figley and McCubben, 1983; Voydanoff, 1983; Voydanoff and Majka, 1988) has identified two basic types of stress. Normative stress is perceived to be the result of transitions that regularly occur in family life (Larson, 1984; McCubben and Patterson, 1983). The other type, the one of interest here, is catastrophic stress, which stems from unanticipated environmental trauma.

Family adaptation is seen as more difficult in catastrophic stress because new patterns have to be acquired to deal with the sudden and unexpected. Unemployment, especially widespread, unpredictable unemployment, is among the catastrophic stresses faced by families (Voydanoff, 1983). Families become demoralized but eventually begin to search out resources with which to cope (Voydanoff and Donnelly, 1988). The "copers" appear to be women, according to a few recent studies of family relationships in times of economic stress (McLloyd, 1989; Elder et al. , 1992). Women endure hardship more calmly and buffer stressful family relationships (Binns and Mars, 1984). Generally, women have been found to have a resilient and constructive approach to human relationships (Hagestad, 1984, 1985). That they are the caretakers from generation to generation has been well documented (Baum and Page, 1991; Horowitz, 1985; Rosenthal, 1985). Women have also been found to have significantly larger social networks and to both give and receive more support than men (Kahn and Antonucci, 1983). In times of stress, informal networks composed of family and friends and formal supports from community institutions and agencies have proved very important in securing emotional comfort and fulfilling family life needs (Atkinson, Liem, and Siem, 1986; Gore, 1978). Focusing on women in households helped to promote a better understanding about their experiences with economic catastrophe and the contributions women made to family adaptation.

EMPLOYMENT, UNEMPLOYMENT, AND TRAINING

The first part of the interviews focused on the unemployment experience and the changes it brought to the households. Before the industrial collapse occurred, the majority of the respondents' families were financially quite comfortable. Paychecks and benefits were generous. Lifestyles declined dramatically when the massive unemployment occurred. According to the women's retrospective responses on a seven-point scale, median household income fell from $25,000 before unemployment to $10,000 in the immediate aftermath. Even when the study was conducted, six years after the peak job losses in 1981 and 1982, the median income remained at $10,000. Although more household members were employed by then, the jobs tended to be low paying, less likely to be full-time, and less likely to include benefits. Some households had to turn to welfare, an option considered highly undesirable by the respondents from the mill towns.

The diminished income led to other problems. One-third of the families lost homes they had owned or were forced to move to less expensive rental housing. Adequate housing maintenance was not affordable, and outmoded appliances could not be replaced. Finding adequate medical care became a nightmare for many families after benefits were lost. Only some families, mostly those with young children, found relief through the medical assistance program. Job training was eagerly sought and at least one member in half of the households sampled enrolled in an education or training program. Unfortunately, however, at the time of the interview, only a small proportion of the enrollees, 10 percent, had found jobs as a result (Baum, Shore, and Fleissner, 1988).

As in battered households, the two most vulnerable groups were blacks and single mothers, black and white. Adult members of the black households were virtually wiped out of the well-paid blue-collar positions where they had had a significant foothold, proportionately more black households had to depend on welfare, and the deprivations around housing for this subgroup of the population were the highest. The households headed by single women, however, were at the bottom of the ladder. Almost none of these women were employed and, to their consternation, some of their teenage children were dropping out of school to try to get jobs. Only in obtaining medical coverage were the two most vulnerable groups somewhat better off. Opportunities for training and education were fairly equally distributed across groups, although younger household members were somewhat more involved regardless of race. Unfortunately, however, none of the population groups had reaped much advantage in acquiring jobs.

SOCIAL COSTS AND SOCIAL SUPPORTS

The lengthiest part of the interviews concentrated on the impact of unemployment on family life and efforts to alleviate psychosocial and material stresses. As is predictable in cases of catastrophic unemployment, the unforeseen trauma demoralized the family lives of most women in the short run. Asked for their retrospective evaluations (on a frequently used five-point scale) of family happiness before unemployment struck and immediately after unemployment, they indicated a huge drop in perceived happiness between pre-unemployment and post-unemployment. Before unemployment, almost nine of ten women (88 percent) judged family life to have been somewhat or very happy. After unemployment almost three-fifths (58.3 percent) of the respondents rated family life as somewhat or very unhappy. Asked again about family happiness at the time of the interview, even though income levels had not actually improved, ratings became significantly more positive. A sizable majority (58.3 percent) of the evaluations were in the somewhat happy to very happy range.

The partial resurgence of perceived happy family lives occurred amid continuing unsatisfactory employment and financial distress. In the generally very flat economy, women were not able to contribute much to family income through increased paid work involvement. In spite of serious efforts to find work or to find more work, the proportion of women working after the mills closed fell from 60 percent to 44.6 percent, and more of these jobs were part-time. Many job seekers gave up fruitless searches to devote their energies to their families and to shoring up resources in other ways. Whether they were working or not, most of the women (between 70 and 75 percent) reported that they still did all or almost all of the major household tasks as well as child care and budgeting. The crisis brought on even more demands. The respondents recounted their efforts to bring family members closer together, to maintain informal support systems, and to access formal services as needed for household maintenance.

Only seven of the marriages ended in divorce, but most families were feeling at least temporarily unbalanced in a suddenly insecure world. Many families did recover at least partially over time, and one method of helping families to become happier again was to "close ranks" to generate a new sense of solidarity. Over half the married women (52 percent) devoted more time to their husbands, and many felt a new sense of closeness (41 percent). An even larger proportion of women said they spent more time with their children (54.8 percent), and all of these respondents felt that closeness to their children had increased. The women admitted that arguments occurred in the family, but in open-ended comments women often said that the arguments were healthy. Family members needed to come to grips with their reduced lifestyles and to try to generate a sense of fairness about distributing the burdens. Most women commented that disrupted family relations were mended through caring efforts. Some women even said that the disastrous unemployment experience brought unexpected benefits in a renewed discovery of the importance of family.

In the social milieu of deprived communities suffering severe and enduring economic depression, maintaining informal social supports would be expected to be difficult. The study women, however, managed to maintain small but staunchly loyal support networks with whom they were in daily or at least weekly contact. Asked to identify the "people closest to you, that is any one you turn to or who can turn to you when support is needed," all respondents named at least one such "closest person," and a large majority (86 percent) named at least two. Attention will focus on the first two since the number naming additional persons after two dropped off sharply. Among the two closest persons identified, about 75 percent were women and almost 80 percent lived in a different household. Family members such as mothers, sisters, and daughters constituted 66 percent of the female closest persons and the remaining 34 percent were female friends. Among the male closest persons, husbands ranked first, followed by fathers and adult sons.

Women were primarily turning to one another in desperate times, and emotional support was the most frequent woman-to-woman gift. Over 90 percent of the respondents said they gave and received emotional support from their female "closest persons." Most of them were considered confidants to whom the respondents could speak openly and trustingly. Because they resided in different households from the study women, yet often shared the same pain, this trust was possible and served as a "safety valve" to allow women to maintain equilibrium at home. Material and practical assistance were also exchanged with the two closest persons, although at much lower rates. Major items were help with transportation, child care, and household matters. In each of these areas and especially in financial assistance, the study women were more likely to receive than to give help, although there was considerable reciprocity. The study women obviously found the patterns of exchange gratifying. Nearly four-fifths (78.7 percent) reported that they were always satisfied with help from closest others. In open-ended comments, closest persons were described as always ready and willing to help, as people who had stood by them in the worst of times and who could always be counted on to "be there." In essence, this is a modified extended family network, composed largely of women, which stretches across households and may, in this way, help to sustain whole communities (Baum, Shore, and Fleissner, 1988, 1993).

The majority of the women respondents had never been faced with the necessity of applying to formal organizations for assistance. Mill town families had been stable and self-supporting for several generations. Some respondents saw applying for help as "begging" and avoided it as long as possible. Approaching formal organizations was a different proposition than turning to relatives and friends. A large majority of the respondents identified themselves as highly religious, and it was to the church relief programs that almost half the women (48.7 percent) turned first. Church offerings, however, were limited, and the majority of respondents (63.6 percent) received assistance from social service agencies. The churches and the social service agencies gave similar types of help, and the women often had to apply to two or more agencies to receive enough help to meet household needs. The most frequently received assistance was food, financial aid, and energy subsidies. Only a small number (12.4 percent) of the respondents applied for mental health services for themselves or, more frequently, for family members.

Most women were satisfied with what they had received, but about two-fifths (40.6 percent) felt that they had received too little or that what they received took too long to obtain. The most dissatisfaction arose with mental health services, where the users complained that help received was for too short a time or that the family members who most needed counseling had not been persuaded to accept help. After all their persistence, almost half the respondents (47.4 percent) reported that they did not receive as much help as they needed, especially with food stamps, medical care, child care, and financial aid. The women reported that the service they most needed was "support groups." Although all had at least one confidant, the need for more exchange with other women in the communities in the economic crisis was their top priority. Some respondents added that men needed special support groups as well.

Probably the most upsetting experience commented upon by the women was being refused public assistance. About two-thirds of the women applied for public assistance when other resources had been exhausted. Public assistance was seen as the "survival" program because it was the only one that supplied the basic necessities of life. Of those who applied, two-fifths (41 percent) were accepted with little delay. But over a quarter (27.4 percent) were accepted only after long and frustrating delays, and the remaining third (31.5 percent) were rejected. Delays and rejections were sometimes accompanied by welfare personnel making demeaning remarks about "people who won't work for a living" (Baum, Shore, and Fleissner, 1988, 1993).

When black families and families headed by single females were compared to other groups here, the black women especially, whether married or not, were likely to have very supportive and reciprocal informal network partners. Although the study women as a whole were very patient and persistent in pursuing help from formal systems, the black women appeared especially resourceful in finding help. Black women were less likely than white women to report that a needed service was not available. While they would definitely have preferred employment opportunities, which they had sought, black women did get more help from churches and service agencies, which offered some compensation.

IN SUMMARY

One hundred and fifty-two women, subdivided by age and race, were interviewed face-to-face at length about their experiences and those of other household members with unemployment. All respondents were residents in households with at least one other family member and in which at least one household member had been unemployed during the six years prior to the study.

One and often more than one member in the study households had lost well-paying jobs and either remained unemployed or eventually secured less well paying jobs with no fringe benefits. Income plummeted from a median household income of $25,000 before unemployment to $10,000 immediately after unemployment. Although more household members again had jobs at the time of the interview, the quality of those jobs is revealed by the median household income's remaining at $10,000. Loss of jobs led to loss of income, which often meant losing one's home or moving to cheaper, less satisfactory rental housing. At best, housing deteriorated because there was no money to make repairs or to replace outmoded appliances. One of the worst deprivations resulting from unemployment and underemployment was the loss of health benefits. Many household members either tried to treat their own illnesses and injuries or rationed their health care severely unless a medical assistance card could be obtained. At least one adult member in half of the 152 households received job or educational training. In the short run, however, training led to employment for only 10 percent of the trainees in these households. Black households and households headed by single women (black or white) were the most likely to have members who became and remained unemployed, and the most likely to have incomes below the poverty line. These were also the households that were suffering disproportionately in housing arrangements, although they were proportionately less likely to be deprived of health care. In access to training, this study found no evidence of discrimination by race or gender. Ageism was apparent, however, in that training opportunities went almost exclusively to those under 30.

Economic catastrophe left demoralized families, and the perceived level of family happiness descended dramatically in the aftermath of massive unemployment in the two mill towns from which the sample was drawn. By the time of the interview, however, happiness flowed back to an unanticipated extent, given the fact that income remained stagnant and the job market lethargic. Women in affected households made contributions to that resurgence by responding to the crisis in several ways. Although the women continued to perform all major household tasks and worked to contribute to the family income via paid employment when the opportunity was found, other demands were placed upon them. Women in the distressed households put additional energies into forming closer relationships with their husbands and, especially, their children. They maintained small but very strong informal support systems, for the most part composed of women in other distressed households. From these other women they received highly reciprocal emotional support that helped to maintain equilibrium in times of high stress. Many practical forms of assistance were also exchanged, although at a somewhat lesser level. Much of the exchange was "all in the family" and suggested that a network of close female relatives and friends was a major source of emotional and practical strength to households in the stricken communities. Interestingly, however, additional support groups was the top-priority service need expressed by the respondents.

The study women, although new to applying to formal organizations for assistance, proved to be capable of finding the resources that they needed to keep their families going. It was, however, an enormous struggle to obtain resources, and many women from families that were clearly sadly deprived found the level of obtained support inadequate. The most serious disappointment was being turned down for the "survival program," public assistance. In the areas of informal and formal supports, black single women seemed to have had the strongest and most giving ties with other female family members and friends. Black single women also proved the most resourceful in obtaining formal organization assistance. Black households and households headed by single females did better than other households in obtaining a precious resource, the medical assistance card.

Chapter 10

Elderly Parents and Their Unemployed Adult Children

Mary H. Page
Myrna Silverman

McKeesport? It changed right in front of your eyes. It used to be a great city . . . shoppers walking three abreast down Walnut Street. Business was booming; plenty of kids . . . schools open. Then, all of a sudden, the city went down from 60,000 to 30,000 people. Now you can't buy a refrigerator, a suit, or a chair here . . . can't go anywhere . . . There's nothing!

Elderly Parent Respondent

A study of the role aging parents played as a resource for their unemployed adult children was conducted by two University of Pittsburgh faculty members, Mary H. Page who teaches family courses at the School of Social Work and works with troubled families in private practice and Myrna Silverman who teaches courses and conducts research on Public Health and Aging at the Graduate School of Public Health (Page and Silverman, 1988).

The study was carried out in McKeesport, the largest of the depressed mill towns in southwestern Pennsylvania. The research had three phases. First, influential leaders from various spheres were identified using a community analysis format, and focused interviews were held with 20 such leaders. The leaders provided background information on the community and also served the very important function of assisting the researchers in identifying community families who would meet specific study criteria.

The second phase of the study was central, involving case studies of 28 families with in-depth, face-to-face interviews with three members of each family: an elderly parent, an employed or unemployed adult child, and a collateral relative. A collateral relative was defined as either a second adult child or as some other third party who could serve as an independent observer of the central parent-child relationship. Most collateral relatives turned out to be employed adult children, so the shift in comparisons went to responses of aging parents to unemployed adult children versus responses of aging parents to employed adult children.

Altogether there were 84 in-depth personal interviews, three for each of the 28 families. Families were subdivided to ensure that there was a fairly even balance between families with and without an unemployed adult child as one of the respondents. The relatively small sample included an overrepresentation of black families in order to pick up any possible differences in caregiving responses by race.

The third phase of the study was a post-data-gathering meeting with the community leaders who were interviewed in the first phase. The investigators shared preliminary findings and sought feedback and recommendations from community leaders. The elderly parents were all long-term residents of McKeesport, a legendary mill town that, according to Hoerr (1988), had for over a century an economic system that provided secure employment and social stability. The parents in the sample were in a unique position to understand what it meant to be laid off periodically and to be dependent on one industry.

The rationale for the study was the necessity to learn more about the responses of the informal social support system to workers who are unemployed for extended periods of time. Critical for this study was the role aging parents played as a resource to their adult children when these children became unemployed. As the lifeline has grown longer, literature on parents of adult children first centered on the emergence of a "roleless role" and loss of status in old age in industrial society (Cowgill and Holmes, 1972).

Recently, there has been a strong emphasis on adult children as caregivers for their aging parents (Baum and Page, 1991; Brody, 1981; Cicerelli, 1981). Elders were seen as included in the "modified extended" family, but on balance as receivers of care rather than as contributors to family resources (Aldous, 1987). More recently, a view of aging shows that medical advances allow most elderly to maintain good health status into what used to be considered fragile old age (Brubaker, 1991). Elderly parents do not necessarily, or even customarily, live in the same household with their adult children, but elders have been found to play a positive role in the mutual aid system the family constitutes (Lowy, 1988; Sussman, 1986). Studies show that family elders invest more in family relationships than do those in younger generations, and that in some instances elders are the primary pillars in the family system of social supports (Bengston and Kuypers, 1971; Smeeding, 1990; Bond and Harvey, 1988). In addition, the "empty nest" that supposedly helped to make elderly parents obsolete is filling up again as adult children find employment, or at least employment at a decent wage, impossible to obtain (Zimmerman, 1988). Questions about the roles played by elderly parents when economic distress decimated a large mill town are addressed in this study.

ECONOMIC DISTRESS IN MCKEESPORT

This research provided an opportunity to compare directly the views of community leaders with those of elderly parent respondents. McKeesport was remembered by the leaders as a thriving, self-sufficient city: "the hub of the valley." Community leaders nostalgically recalled the 1950s and 1960s, when high school graduates readily found good jobs in the mills. At the time of the study, leaders were aware that younger residents were preparing to leave or had already left. Most admitted that they did not anticipate that the city's largest plant would close and that they were stunned when it did. The city had already begun to decline physically due to the loss of the downtown stores to shopping malls. The decline accelerated with the exodus of the unemployed, the erosion of the tax base, and the consequent cutting of services.

A major concern expressed by community leaders centered on housing. Losses in businesses, factories, and mom-and-pop stores produced unemployed persons who left the area to seek employment elsewhere. There was a racial component as well as a class component in the resulting population change in McKeesport. As the leaders saw it, some white residents left large houses that were costly to heat and maintain, and blacks from other areas bought them, often doubling up with other families in order to manage the costs.

Property values declined sharply following the closing of the mills. A new business evolved due to the increase in the aging population and the declining youth population. Owners of large homes, unable to sell at what they considered a fair price, took advantage of the increased numbers of frail elderly in the city to open personal care and nursing homes. An elementary school, which had been closed, was bought by a local businessman and converted to a personal care home. These new enterprises were not sufficient to keep McKeesport afloat. The exodus of families from McKeesport affected other social institutions, such as churches, small businesses, and physical and mental health clinics. Residents whose parents and grandparents had attended ethnic churches in the city now attended whatever church was in their neighborhood, community leaders said, and as a result ethnic ties were weakened. The consensus among community leaders was that chronic unemployment also adversely affected family relationships. The pervasive view was that parents and grandparents were sacrificing for their families while adult children no longer had the patience and money to care for elderly parents and expected the government to provide nursing home care. The community leaders agreed that the elderly in McKeesport had ample services available, if they were still living outside of nursing homes.

While community leaders and aging parents shared similar observations about the changes in McKeesport, the elders expressed a greater sense of pain than was characteristic of the community officials. Very high on the list of concerns for the elderly were crime, vandalism, personal safety, and property abandonment. These factors interfered with free movement around the city, and created real difficulties in participating in service programs located in the downtown area. In their eyes, the once thriving, booming city center was now a "ghost town" or "death valley." Older parents were fearful of leaving their homes at night. Even in the daytime some went out with trepidation and only when necessary. Services for the elderly may have been present, but were not accessible under such conditions.

Like the community leaders, the elderly parents recalled better times and lamented the dwindling resources in the community and the dampened community spirit. The elderly respondents seemed more angry about what had happened. The closing of the mills was perceived as a betrayal of the community, and local officials and other business enterprises came in for their share of blame. Parents sometimes even were upset with their own children for not trying hard enough to find jobs in the area. Other respondents, however, saw positive outcomes despite adversity, such as families growing closer together and informal networks growing even stronger. The elderly parents as a group certainly intended to remain in McKeesport and to be involved in the community as far as possible. They had long-term attachments to religious institutions and voluntary groups, as well as to family, friends, and neighbors. There was also the sense that McKeesport was still home: "Where else would I live?" said one respondent.

SOCIAL COSTS AND SOCIAL SUPPORTS

The data from the elderly parent/adult child interviews revealed a considerable reliance on elderly parents when adult children became unemployed. That the family is a source of help in times of trouble has been well documented. There were also economic factors inherent in the depressed mill towns that may have made it easier for adult children to turn to their elderly parents. Many younger respondents felt that old people were receiving more and better services than the unemployed and so could afford to help. The majority of older parents in this sample tended to be relatively self-sufficient. They were not heavily dependent on family and friends to maintain their households. At the same time, there was solid evidence of a "family presence" in the lives of the elderly respondents. Collectively, the 28 elderly parents had 111 adult children and numerous grandchildren. Seventy-five percent of the respondents reported daily or weekly contact with one or more of their children who lived nearby or in the same household. Such regular contacts suggested ongoing reciprocal social support in which small services in response to mutual needs made formal requests for help unnecessary under most circumstances.

In the sensitive area of asking for and receiving help, the data showed some interesting similarities and differences between the two generations. Both elderly parents and adult children, for example, saw themselves as more likely to give help than receive help from others. Both groups also characterized themselves as hesitant to ask for help.

If and when respondents saw themselves as seeking help, they viewed themselves as most likely to turn to their families. In emergencies, for example, elderly parents were twice as likely to go to family as to neighbors and friends. Both employed and unemployed adult children said that they were three times as likely to go to elderly parents as to anyone else in emergencies. Thus, whether employed or unemployed, adult children were equally likely to turn to their parents in a crisis. In terms of offering assistance, parents responded on the basis of perceived needs (although they claimed to treat all their adult children the same). Aging parents, the findings showed, tended to adapt to crises and served as a major support, rather than a minor one, to their adult children beset by job loss, unemployment, and underemployment.

From the analysis of the data, several patterns and themes emerged to produce five family types. Each family type is a composite profile of similar families rather than any particular family in the sample. The typology subsumes all 28 families studied and is based on the organization of the family, including the work histories of the aging parents and the gender of the principal wage earner prior to retirement. The five family types are described briefly below:

Type 1   *The Traditional Family.* Retired father; mother never worked; adult children hard hit by mill closing; adult children have unstable employment.

Type 2   *The Contemporary Two-Paycheck Family.* Forced retirement of father who seeks part-time work; mother supplements income; chronic unemployment of adult children.

Type 3   *The Independent Family.* Planned retirement of father; mother never worked; adult children employed and support themselves.

Type 4   *The Emerging Single-Female-Head-of-Household Family.* Single mother who entered work late in life due to death, separation, or illness of spouse; adult children may or may not have stable employment.

Type 5   *The Unemployed Family.* Single-mother head of household; never worked; may be a welfare recipient; unemployed adult children.

Most previous studies have described the elderly primarily as recipients of social support, especially from their adult children. This study suggests that when adult children are chronically unemployed or underemployed, new patterns of exchanging social support emerge in which the responsibility shifts to older generations. Under ordinary economic conditions, the older the parents are in years, the more resources flow from the adult child to the elderly. However, in this study, the situation was reversed for unemployed adult children, since elderly parents willingly shared their limited resources with their children. Moreover, elderly parents seemed to be even more willing to extend themselves to adult children when they themselves had undergone hardships. Most parents stated that they would never want to see their adult children or their grandchildren go hungry, go without shelter, or live in desperate need.

Reciprocity and family supportive responses emerged as important to all five types of family systems identified in the study. The analysis of the data performed by grouping older adults and their children into five types, based on the gender of the principal older-generation parent, illustrated several subthemes. All five family types provided extensive and varied support services between the generations. Where the members of the older generation had themselves experienced unemployment, however, the quantity and type of services differed from family types where there had been no experience with unemployment in the prior generation. Where no experience with unemployment had occurred, discretionary services such as funds for parties or for college education for the grandchildren were prominent. Where there had been experience, the services exchanged were more basic and necessary for survival, such as housing and emotional support in the troubling situation.

Regardless of family type, unemployed adult children were not denied a place to live in the parental home, even when the situation caused stress for older adults accustomed to having their homes to themselves. But there were differences among family types in the ability to cope with the pressures of crowding. In cases where the older adults had experienced chronic unemployment or layoffs, they were more understanding and felt less stress than in families where older adults had had uninterrupted work histories.

Both black and white families provided similar types of support services and expressed similar positive attitudes toward supporting their unemployed adult children. As in other studies in this part, however, black families were more likely to be disadvantaged. (See Chapter 8.) Yet despite lowered household incomes and meager resources, black families continued to support their unemployed adult children fully as completely as white families. Another group found to have the most severe economic problems, families headed by both black and white single women, also managed to provide needed resources to their unemployed adult children, although, in some cases, this took considerable skill, energy, and sacrifice.

IN SUMMARY

Page and Silverman carried out an unusual design in investigating the relationships between aging parents and their adult children in times of high economic distress and unemployment. McKeesport, the largest of the depressed mill towns in southwestern Pennsylvania, was the research site. The first research phase contained focused interviews with community leaders who also helped the researchers to select suitable families to fulfill study criteria for respondents.

Interviews with community leaders showed some dissonance between their perceptions and those of the elderly parent respondents. Although both groups shared a sense of change, loss, and deprivation, the community leaders were more optimistic about the future, viewing McKeesport as a viable community with supportive services for the elderly well in place. Older respondents, by contrast, saw themselves as trapped in deteriorating neighborhoods and unable to move about freely because they feared for their safety.

Elderly parents planned to stay where they were, but their sense of anger and alienation was strong.

The data showed that support services for the two generations of interest in the study came primarily from family and friends, although the church was mentioned frequently as a source of comfort. The higher visibility and recognition given to informal supports by both elderly parents and their adult children was due in part to lack of awareness of formal services as well as to fears associated with a changing community. In all five family types the family was the major source of support in times of need for both generations. Adult children overwhelmingly turned to aging parents for help. The parents responded to their needs, especially when the adult children were unemployed. The retirement-age parents in this study had to draw upon pensions, benefit plans, or part-time work to assure that their unemployed adult children and their families survived. Those elderly parents who had themselves undergone unstable employment or layoffs earlier in their lives were more likely to find making sacrifices, including sharing their homes, less stressful than parents who had not undergone such hardships.

Black elderly parents, again the most likely to be in straitened circumstances, nevertheless managed to help their needy children. So, in fact, did single female aging parents, although they had the fewest resources of all to share.

Chapter 11

Steeltown Fathers: Raising Children in an Era of Industrial Decline

Phyllis D. Coontz
Judith A. Martin
Edward W. Sites

When I think about the way this society forced men in my father's generation to be completely responsible for their families, it makes me furious. . . My father took that on himself because that's what all fathers did then. As a result, my mother didn't really know much about the working world. She had to find out the hard way. . . . The whole situation was terrible. It was a bad way to organize a family's survival.

Joan de Lancy,
from *Falling from Grace*
by Katherine S. Newman, 1988, p. 119

The economic changes of the 1980s had a profound impact on families in the region, especially among those whose livelihood

---

The research for the analysis reported here was supported by a grant from the Staunton Farm Foundation, Pittsburgh, PA.

These fathers were randomly drawn from the Coles Directory on the basis of five criteria: the presence of a child < eleven years old living in the household; the father or another adult male living in the home caring for the child(ren); having lost a job since 1980; current employment status; and willingness to participate in the study.

depended on heavy industry. For the Pittsburgh region, some of the changes that occurred may be viewed as improvement, such as the emergence of a more diversified economic base and a cleaner environment. But for those who lost their jobs when the steel industry collapsed, the changes from economic restructuring were destructive. Employment serves as an anchor for economic, social, and personal stability. Thus, the loss of a job not only affects the individual worker, but also his/her relationships with others, particularly family relationships. Researchers since the Great Depression have observed that the uncertainty brought about by large-scale unemployment and marginal employment is a major reason why family relations deteriorate (Angell, 1936; Bakke, 1940; Komarovsky, 1938; Cavan and Ranck, 1938; Larson, 1984; Scholzman, 1979; Liem and Liem, 1979).

The experiences of families who did not relocate, but remained in the region facing uncertainties brought about by economic decline are at once poignant, but also instructive. They reveal much about the difficulties and struggles these families endured, but also draw attention to the myriad ways that these families adapted to their new and changing circumstances.

This chapter focuses on families with young children and looks at the impact that unemployment had on family roles, particularly the provider, homemaker, and child care roles. The analysis described here is based on the responses of 516[1] fathers living in 43 different communities located in Allegheny County (these were largely steel mill towns surrounding the city of Pittsburgh). We deliberately divided the original sample into two groups of fathers, those who experienced major job loss (N=248) and those who had not experienced job loss (N=268) so that we could compare the two groups and better analyze the effects of job loss. A subsample of 101 partners of these fathers were also interviewed to complete a portrait of family life. The study was conducted over a two-and-one-half-year period, with data gathering concluding in 1989. In this chapter we discuss general findings for the whole sample and present a more detailed analysis of the subsample of 101 fathers and mothers.

When the 516 fathers of young children were interviewed, 8.9 percent were then without employment and another 8.5 percent were working only part-time. Forty-eight percent of the 516 fathers had experienced at least one major job loss since 1980. This was at a time when much of the region was experiencing robust recovery, and the official unemployment rate of the Pittsburgh area was down to 4.6 percent.

Reported were alarming rates of poverty, especially among non-white (largely black) families. One-half of the non-white families and one-seventh of the white families had incomes below $1,000 per month. At least one-fourth of the fathers who had been unemployed had received some form of public assistance after exhausting their unemployment compensation rights. Nearly one-fourth of those interviewed reported that they were enjoying "much less" household income than five years before. Most of the fathers were members of stable nuclear families, and 56 percent reported that their wives worked at least part-time. In a significant number of these families, both parents worked outside of the home during the same hours, including 30 percent in which both were out of the home working after 6 p.m.

PAST FINDINGS ON FATHERS

Research from the Great Depression era of the 1930s by Komarovsky (1987) revealed that unemployment had the potential to make a solid relationship stronger and a shaky relationship weaker. She found that unemployed fathers' behavior deteriorated in 37 percent of the cases studied. Deterioration was defined as greater emotional instability, lower morale, increased irritability, and increased drinking. The families which faired better were those that were highly adaptable. As might be expected, adaptability was contingent on a variety of factors. Quite often unemployment necessitated familial role changes that produced marital strain and conflict. Bakke (1940) summed up the child care situation for Depression era unemployed fathers by noting that fathers lacked the energy and patience to deal effectively with child care responsibilities, and consequently did not participate in the care of their children.

The need to examine the effect of unemployment on family roles today is strongly suggested by both changes in the structure of the family and its functioning since the Depression era, and by the extent of the problem of unemployment. Most economists and labor experts agree that high levels of unemployment are a permanent feature of modern-day society (Joint Economic Committee of Congress, 1986; Seaberry, 1986, Nash, 1987). In 1984, 7 million children in four million families in the United States had at least one unemployed adult in the household. Of these 7 million children, 3 million had an unemployed mother, 3.4 million had an unemployed father, and one-half million had two unemployed parents (Moen, 1983).

The children of unemployed parents are particularly vulnerable to the effects of unemployment because they are dependent on their parents for physical care and social and psychological development. What was learned from the Depression era research is that unemployment can affect the parents' capacity to care for the needs of their children. In addition to its effect on parental responsibilities, more recent research has found that unemployment affects personal and martial relationships as well (Komarovsky, 1967). The quality and stability of the marital relationship in turn has important implications for family functioning.

People cope with major life stress in many ways. Often, the impact of stress from job loss can be reduced if the unemployed worker has access to support from family, friends, or relatives (Gore, 1978). Social supports provide a person under stress with the sense that others understand and care about what has happened, thereby mediating the stress.

If the structure of the family during the last one hundred years is examined, the single most significant change that has affected family life has been the change in women's roles, particularly from homemakers to wage earners. This shift in role responsibilities has important implications for the functioning of the family as well as the availability of wives/mothers to care for family needs. While women have always worked and while their work has varied by race and class, their labor has been confined principally to the domestic or agricultural arenas. Since the 1890s, however, women have increased and diversified their participation in the nonagricultural, nonfamilial, paid labor force.

In 1890, fewer than 5 percent of all married women in the United States worked outside the home for wages and salaries (Ferree, 1984). By 1947, one out of five married women (or 20 percent) was employed in the paid labor force. The proportion of married working women rose to one in four by 1960 and by 1980 the proportion was one out of two married women (DHHS, 1987). Today, this has probably risen to about six out of ten. More important, perhaps, is that three quarters of the women who are now working, work full-time, and the income that they earn is instrumental to the financial well-being of their families (Moen, 1983). While the enormous increase in the number of married women working in the nondomestic/nonagricultural labor force is the result of larger structural changes in our economy necessitating two incomes, it has nevertheless produced major changes in the way families function. An obvious impact has been in the amount of time that women have available to devote to child care and domestic responsibilities. Although today more women work than ever before, they continue to assume primary responsibility for domestic chores and child care. Hochschild and Machung (1990), provided evidence that working women actually work two jobs: one in the marketplace and one at home.

Unemployment cuts in two directions. It has the potential to reduce a father's involvement in child care by creating paralyzing additional burdens or stresses on the family from the loss of income. It also has the potential to increase a father's involvement by providing time and opportunities for involvement. There is much evidence that when given the opportunity to take on child-rearing responsibilities, few men choose to do so (Chang and Deinard, 1982). The more traditionally oriented a man is, the more conflict he experiences over assuming what is perceived as "women's work" (Kohn, 1989). Moreover, dissatisfaction or conflict over increased child care responsibilities has important implications for the harmony of the family environment, the care of children, and the marital relationship.

PITTSBURGH AREA STUDY

Since the impact of unemployment on parenting and family life was a major consideration for the study reported here, the sample of 516 fathers was drawn from census tracts in which a third or more of the workers were employed in durable manufacturing industries in 1980. Seventy-one census tracts in Allegheny County were found to fit this profile. Allegheny County contains the City of Pittsburgh, and a checkerboard of old industrial boroughs and younger suburban townships. All of the 71 target census tracts with their concentrations of blue-collar workers turned out to be in the boroughs and townships, none in the City. From these census tracts, a random sample was selected and the residents were contacted by telephone via trained interviewers.

Repeated calls were made at staggered times of the day to ensure reaching as many of those in the sample as possible. A total of 11,744 households were contacted of which 15 percent met the criterion of having at least one child under 12 and a male who provided a significant amount of the care of the young child(ren). Of the 1,816 who met the profile, 43 percent declined to be interviewed. Eventually 516 of the 1,034 fathers who were potentially willing to participate were interviewed face-to-face in their homes. These were scattered throughout forty-three communities in Allegheny County, all of which were outside the City of Pittsburgh.

As mentioned earlier, a subsample of 101 of the fathers' partners was randomly selected for interviewing. While data on the 516 fathers are reported here (see Table 11.1 for a general description of the occupational background of the total sample), much of this chapter is devoted to examining the responses of the 101 couples.

Background of 101 Couples

Age

The mean ages of the 101 fathers and their partners were 35.5 and 33.9 years, respectively. The range for the men was 21 to 62 years and for the women, 19 to 59 years. The high ages result because a number of men who passed the original telephone screen as providers of child care for young children were found to be grandfathers. Since multigeneration families in which men function as parenting partners, though not marital partners, provide a more comprehensive view of the roles of men in child care, the grandfathers were kept in the study.

Educational Levels

These were quite high. Many more men (15.7 percent) and women (12.4 percent) completed vocational education than the

Table 11.1
Characteristics of Fathers
General Information
(Total Sample of 516)

	Mean Years
Age	36.3
Age When Married	24.9
Partner's Age	33.9
Experienced Major Job Loss	48.1%
Number of Children Under 12	1.74

Occupation
(Subsample of 462 Employed Fathers)

Classification*	Percent
Labor/Menial Service Workers	4.1
Unskilled Workers	9.5
Machine Operators/Semi-Skilled Workers	14.3
Skilled Manual Workers, Craftsmen, and Very Small Business Owners	31.4
Clerical, Sales Workers, and Small Business Owners	3.4
Technicians and Semiprofessionals	19.7
Managers, Minor Professionals, and Entertainers	8.0
Administrators, Proprietors of Medium-Sized Businesses, and Lesser Professionals	4.8
High Executives, Proprietors of Large Businesses, and Major Profs.	4.8
	100.0

* Adopted from August B. Hollingshead, "Four Factor Index of Social Status," working paper distributed by the author, Dept. of Sociology, Yale University (1975).

Major Job Loss 1980-1989
(Subsample of 248)

Reason	Percent
Plant/Company Closed or Moved	38.2
Slack Work	39.7
Position/Shift Abolished	19.8
Self-Operated Business Failed	2.3
	100.0

national average of 1.8 percent. In addition, more men and women completed at least some college education than both the Pennsylvania and United States averages (DHHS, 1987). Of the men, 4.1 percent completed less than a high school education but 77.9 percent had completed at least an associate degree. For the women only 2.8 percent did not complete high school and 82.8 percent had completed at least an associate degree. Roughly, an equal number of men (13.8 percent) and women (11 percent) had completed college.

Household Composition

The subsample of parenting partners interviewed for this study lived in households with a mean of 4.13 persons. Most families (90.7 percent) lived in a house and three-fourths of these families owned or were purchasing their homes. A small number (2 percent) reported that they were living with someone else.

About one-fourth of the families had only one child; 45 percent had two children; 28 percent had three children; and 3 percent had four children. The men's and women's enumerations of children differed slightly because the question was posed as one of household composition; a tiny fraction (fewer than 1 percent) of the fathers provided significant care for their children but did not live with them. More women (8.9 percent) than men (5.9 percent) had children from a previous marriage. As might be expected, many more women than men had children from previous marriages living with them.

Marital Relationships

Most (97 percent) of the parenting partners were married to each other. The mean ages at which they were married to their present partner were 24.7 years for the men and 23 years for the women. These were highly stable marriages, having lasted an average of eleven years by the time of the study. Previous marriages were reported by 10.9 percent of the men and 8.9 percent of the women. Divorce rates, below the U.S. and Pennsylvania averages, may have been an artifact of the sampling procedures. Stable, ethnic communities and families with strong religious ties, a tradition in Pittsburgh's industrial towns, may also be influential factors.

Religion

Of the respondents to this survey 53.5 percent of the men and 55.5 percent of the women reported being Catholic. More men (6 percent) than women (2 percent) reported no religious affiliation. These rates for no affiliation are much lower than in the general population. Affiliation and the support of religious groups were reported to be of considerable significance by the respondents.

Father's Employment

At the time of the interview, two-thirds of the men held full-time jobs; only 8.3 percent were not in the work force because they were disabled or retired.

While most worked for someone else, there was a small percentage, under 15 percent, who were engaged in self-employment, either full-time or part-time. Less than 7 percent were enrolled in a formal program of education, and approximately one of five was looking for work. The job seekers were employed and unemployed persons. Most of the employed fathers were craftsmen, technicians, and machine operators. There were a handful of professionals.

For those who went through a major job loss (MJL) and reemployment, more than half experienced a shift in the nature of their employment. For one-third, their first employment after MJL was in a lower status job. However, nearly one-fourth (23.7 percent) found new employment of a higher status, and 42.9 percent found employment at the same status level, though not necessarily in the same type of job.

In addition to those who sustained MJL, many of those who changed jobs (23.3 percent), experienced unemployment for some period. The respondents reported a mean of 2.12 different full-time and .52 part-time jobs since 1980. A number of respondents did not describe returning to the same employer after a lay-off as separate employment. Consequently, it is probable that these figures are measuring employer changes rather than job changes, with the latter likely to be more numerous.

In total, the fathers spent nearly one-fifth of their time during the period from January 1980 to August, 1988 (104 months) being unemployed. For those who experienced MJL, the impact was even more profound. In a period of 104 months, nearly three-fourths of the MJL fathers changed employment. Only 28.7 percent did not experience any job change during these years.

For the half of the fathers who experienced a MJL, the mean number of months unemployed from just that one job loss was 10.8 months. Some had more than one major job loss by the definition used in the study, but each father for whom this was the case specified which job loss he considered his major one. Sometimes this loss was not the one leading to the longest period of unemployment.

During MJL, 90.7 percent of the fathers received unemployment compensation benefits and 62.9 of those receiving them exhausted their entitlements. Sixty percent of those who had a MJL considered moving to a different city or county, almost exactly the same percentage as had fully used their unemployment compensation entitlement.

INCOME AND ECONOMIC WELL-BEING

A somewhat mixed picture emerges from the assessments made by the respondents of their economic situations. The women in the subsample of 101 tended to perceive a brighter situation in comparison to five years ago. More than 68 percent believed that their income was "a little higher" or "much higher" than before, while less than 58 percent of the men saw this much improvement. However there was agreement among about one-fourth of the fathers and mothers that their incomes were "a little less" or "much less" than five years ago. Most of these were in the "much less" category. (See Table 11.2.)

However, when asked about their actual dollar monthly income, the women presented a somewhat less optimistic scene. Their mean reported monthly income was $1,001 to $1,400 per month, which is below or close to the poverty level for families of the size represented in this sample. Indeed more than one-fourth of the women said that their monthly family income was below $1,000. The fathers on the other hand estimated a mean monthly income of $1,401 to $1,800. It is notable that the men and women tended to agree on their family income at the lower levels while men gave more optimistic reports in the upper ranges. Table 11.3 lists the comparisons.

Table 11.2
Perceptions of Changes in Last Five Years
(n=101 Fathers and 101 Partners)

Income Level	Percent of Fathers	Percent of Partners
Much higher	21.9	18.9
A little higher	35.8	49.8
About the same	15.8	6.9
A little less	6.9	8.9
Much less	19.6	15.5
Totals	100.0	100.0

Table 11.3
Total Monthly Family Income
Contrasting Estimates
(n-100 Fathers and 101 Partners)

Monthly Income	Percent of Fathers	Percent of Partners
$0 - 200	1.0	1.0
201 - 400	0.0	3.0
401 - 600	4.0	4.0
601 - 800	4.0	5.0
801 - 1000	11.0	12.9
1001 - 1400	14.0	15.7
1401 - 1800	16.0	20.8
1801 - 2200	18.0	20.8
2201 - 2600	16.0	9.9
2601 - or more	16.0	6.9
Totals	100.0	100.0

Income differences by race were significant. One-half of the 53 nonwhite fathers in the full sample of 516 reported total family income of less than $1,000, while only 14.7 percent of 460 white fathers reported incomes that low. This indicates that at least half of the non-white families lived in poverty. Just 21.2 percent of the minority families had incomes above the mean. Moreover there were *stark racial differences* in the extent to which the family situations have changed in the last five years. More than half of the nonwhite families (52.9 percent) reported having less income than five years prior, while only about one-fourth (26.5 percent) of white families reported less income. As might be expected, having had a major job loss in the period 1980-1988 was strongly correlated with poverty. While 13 percent of all families had incomes below $1,000 per month, 22 percent of those who had experienced a major job loss had such incomes.

After unemployment compensation was exhausted, at least a fourth of those with MJL found it necessary to obtain some form of public assistance. Because they referred to this aid by different names (e.g., public assistance, welfare, cash grant, AFDC) and because some families received more than one form of assistance (e.g., food stamps and cash assistance) the unduplicated number of recipients is uncertain.

In all their full-and part-time jobs, the sample of 516 reported that their partners worked 30.5 hours in a normal week. The work hours of the partners were about evenly distributed between daylight (47.5 percent) and late or combined shifts (52.5 percent). This pattern is identical to that of the men. Of the families in which both men and women were employed, over half worked the same shift, approximately evenly distributed between day and night shifts. Economic necessities, school hours of children, seniority, and other factors undoubtedly helped determine the shifts worked. But in about half of the families in which both parents worked they were away from home while school age children were *not* in school. This means that the care of their young children was a major matter requiring attention. The women partners held lower status jobs in the same proportion as men, but a larger percentage had high status positions.

Two groups of families, both numerous, seem to emerge from these data. One group has not experienced unemployment or major job loss; its members have adequate incomes and in general present themselves as secure and relatively strong. The second group has experienced devastating losses since 1980. This predominantly blue-collar group has struggled with major job loss, unemployment underemployment, and other stresses. Many are financially worse off than before, with nearly one-fourth of all those who experienced major job loss now living in poverty. For nonwhite families, the disparity was even more skewed. The economic changes of the past dozen years have created a have and have-not split society in Pittsburgh's industrial communities.

PARENTS AND CHILD CARE

As Mary Jo Bane and David Ellwood (1989) describe for the country as a whole, families in the Pittsburgh area relied primarily on the immediate family to provide the bulk of child care resources for their children. Mothers are most likely to care for their children on a daily basis, and, when they are working or otherwise unavailable, fathers are most likely to take over this job. In 77 percent of the households surveyed here, this task was shared primarily between the father and his partner.

For the families in which a major job loss was experienced, there was quite close agreement between parenting partners on who provided the care of their young children prior to the father's job loss. Fathers provided little, their partners provided most. Relatives and others provided some, and paid day care was almost never used. Fathers reported their partners provided 68.6 percent of the child care, and the partners themselves reported providing 76.3 percent of the care before job loss. Use of outside resources will be discussed below. Fathers reported themselves providing only 5.7 percent of the care.

Perceptions of who provided child care, and to what extent after the father's major job loss, do not agree quite as closely. Both fathers and their partners acknowledge sizable increases in the child care provided by fathers after major job loss, though they do not agree completely. Fathers reported their provisions of care increased from 5.7 percent to 48.6 percent and that their partners' provision of care dropped from 68.6 percent to 25.7 percent. Their partners, on the other hand, reported the fathers increase was only to 26.3 percent and their own decrease from 76.3 percent to 21.1 percent. Both parents attributed much of the child care after the father's major job loss to a shared arrangement. Wives reported an increase in this pattern from 5.3 percent to 39.5 percent.

Clearly, there was a marked increase in the amount of care fathers provided their children after major job loss. In fact both partners agree that after major job loss, fathers provided more of the child care than their partners. It would appear that when fathers lost their jobs, many partners obtained employment and fathers provided much of the needed child care. However, this does not necessarily indicate long-term change. While fathers increased the time that they devoted to child care immediately after their major job loss, there are indications this declined, perhaps sharply, after a transition period. A much closer examination of the attitudes of fathers and their partners as well as their actual performance of a variety of daily household and child care tasks is needed to fully understand these results.

OTHER PARENT ACTIVITIES

With the recent "discovery" of the fathers' direct role in child rearing (Lamb 1982), attention is beginning to be paid to his paternal role. However, available studies are still few in number. As a result, basic questions about fatherhood have yet to be answered.

Most parenting literature written over the last thirty years has assumed that the role of fathers was nominal in child rearing. The literature has described the father as primarily the family breadwinner and as a critical source of support for his wife, with the latter responsible for child care and nurturing. Because fathers were viewed as *less immediately important,* their behavior and attitudes were not studied. Only mothers have traditionally been included in research on "parenthood". In fact, the word "parent" and "mother" became virtually synonymous. Fathers were shadowy background figures in a child's early life, their direct impact on the child unclear and relatively unexplored. Only their indirect impact as wage earner was recognized.

Today, more attention is being given to the male parent. Fathers are beginning to be viewed as having a role in child rearing that is sometimes overlapping and sometimes complementary to that of the mother (LaRossa and LaRossa, 1981). Widening interest in the father role has been stimulated, in part, by broad social expectations that fathers should be more invested in child rearing. But most recent literature finds the imbalance still there (LaRossa and LaRossa, 1981).

Although parents generally agreed about each others' involvement in child care, the greatest discrepancy in the overall responses of these fathers and their partners related to their perceptions about disciplining their children. A substantial number of men (39 percent) see themselves as carrying greater responsibility for this job; however, only 19 percent of the women described the men as more involved. Forty-one percent of the women described themselves as carrying more weight here; only 24 percent of the men agreed in this perception. Both men and women agreed that fathers participate in child rearing and that they do so to a substantial extent in some areas, notably moral guidance and play.

The Pittsburgh study looked at parents' sense of attachment to children, the extent to which they felt their child care responsibilities restricted their other activities, their evaluation of their capacity to do a competent job as a parent, and their perceptions of their child(ren)'s responsiveness to their guidance and caretaking efforts.

While women consistently scored very positive, one attachment item where women's responses were less positive than men's was with the statement, "Sometimes my youngest child does things that bother me just to be mean." Because parents who use excessive force in disciplining their children tend to perceive their children as purposefully defying them, such a response can indicate greater vulnerability among the women than the men in this sample. Generally, fathers described more attachment difficulty, but mothers found their parenting role more restricting. Men and women provided surprisingly uniform positive responses on their ability to do a competent job. On child responsiveness women described far more difficulty than men with the statement, "When I do things for my youngest child, I get the feeling that my efforts are not appreciated very much."

These parenting findings describe a traditional group of fathers and mothers, parents who see child care as more often the woman's job than the man's. Day-to-day child care responsibilities and comforting the child are seen by both as falling within the province of mothers' duties. It is clear, despite widespread social agreement that children need to be more engaged with their fathers, these male parents continue to play a limited role in their children's lives.

In general, the relative delegation of parenting responsibilities between men and women is reinforced by beliefs that child care responsibilities should be distributed in this way. Both mothers and fathers also believe the pattern of their child caretaking has not interfered with their ability to get close to their children, and they feel competent in their caretaking roles.

Perhaps the most disturbing finding is that a significant number of fathers and mothers find themselves in serious difficulty in that they do not feel close to their youngest child and do not find their child's behavior reinforcing or rewarding. Because the building of basic trust is considered a cornerstone of the parent-child relationship (Erikson, 1994), we are concerned about the long-term consequences of this disconnection for some young children in these Pittsburgh area families.

A history of major job loss during the 1980s was not associated with current parental involvement, according to the men and women in this Pittsburgh study. However, for the fathers in the sample, there was a strong connection between the extent of engagement in parenting activities and current employment. Moving from unemployment to part-time to full-time and on to "overload" (full- and part-time) status was associated with decreasing involvement in routine child care tasks and child comforting. As fathers worked more, their partners took on more of these responsibilities. Moreover, once a father took on any job, his partner engaged in more play behavior and did more moral education with his children as well; if he were unemployed, he participated in more of these tasks with his partner or did more of them himself-at least in the beginning of his unemployment period.

Neither the fathers nor their partners described any consistent association between their socio-economic status and the level of their engagement in child care. However, as men moved up the social class ladder, they felt more attached to, more reinforced by, and more competent in caring for their children.

OUTSIDE CHILD CARE RESOURCES

Recent changes in the patterns of employment among mothers highlight the importance of examining the types of child care resources available to the family. Of interest is whether outside child care arrangements were regularly used by these families, the extent to which families relied on paid baby sitters or day care centers, and the shifts that occurred in these arrangements as a result of a father's major job loss.

The most widely-used outside resource for these families was extended family members, especially grandparents. As a second resource for these families was extended family members, especially grandparents. As a third resource, parents turned to friends and neighbors for child care support. This pattern was evident both for routine and emergency care. Paid child care (sitter, day care) was rarely used, and there was equally little recourse to using a child's sibling for care or leaving the child home alone. The importance of adults in the immediate and extended family is evident in these results.

Very few fathers (8.9 percent) said that they would prefer any changes in these child care arrangements; among the small number who did, a clear majority (60 percent) wished that their partner, the child's grandparent, or they themselves could be more available for care. Only eleven men in the entire sample of 516 said that they wished they could place their child in day care.

A number of families in the sample (18.4 percent) had used a "swap" system to obtain child care by taking turns with another family; only 4 percent had ever paid for child care through a "barter" system-providing services or transportation in return for care.

INVOLVEMENT OF FATHERS
IN HOUSEHOLD TASKS

According to the literature, the relative involvement of men and women in household chores, such as cleaning and grocery shopping, follows the same pattern depicted for involvement in child care tasks. The traditional division of labor is evident: mom carries the heaviest load. Robinson (1988) found that women commit twenty hours per week on the average to domestic tasks, while men spend less than ten hours on these chores. During the past 25 years, men in the USA have taken on added responsibility for household tasks. In 1965, women spent more than five times as much time in domestic labor as men, while in 1985 they spent only twice the number of hours, according to Robinson (1988). However, the women's sphere of responsibility has also widened. They are now far more involved in what was once considered "men's housework," activities such as yard clean-up and bill paying (Coverman and Shelly, 1986).

Comparing the extent of men's involvement in household chores before they experienced major job loss with their involvement today reveals similar patterns for Pittsburgh area families. Before major job loss, fathers were less involved in making meals, grocery shopping, doing dishes, and cleaning the house, than they are presently. For bill paying, women's involvement in this chore is greater today than in the past. Men's involvement in "man's work" has changed little over these years. However, while men described themselves as doing more housework, women's assessments of the fathers' involvement in such chores changed very little over the years, suggesting differing perceptions of mothers and fathers about this issue. Black respondents reported slightly more shared housework than white respondents.

THE EFFECT OF INTIMATE
AND CONFIDING RELATIONSHIPS

Although the economic impact from job loss generally has been lessened since the Depression by a variety of "safety-net programs," such as unemployment compensation, food stamps, Medicaid, housing subsidies, and other forms of public assistance, unemployment is still financially distressing, particularly when it is caused by structural changes in the economy.

As described in previous pages, manufacturing was the economic mainstay of the area and central to Pittsburgh's history, growth, and development. When the steel and other heavy industries collapsed, thousands of high paying, unionized jobs were permanently lost, and the whole economic base of the area was transformed. Approximately the same number of jobs in the collapse were replaced by 1990, but the skills, pay, and benefits of the new jobs were qualitatively different. For those who had once earned a "better than average" living in industry, earnings from the replacement jobs were often much lower and involved substantial losses in benefits. And for many others, replacement jobs were either never found or were only temporary or part-time.

But financial hardships are only part of the story. Job loss can be devastating in other important ways. For example, research has consistently found that job loss affects the emotional stability and physical health of individuals and erodes family functioning (Gore, 1978). Work is a fundamental part of most people's lives. It gives purpose and meaning to life and provides a basis for self worth (Jahoda, 1979). Job loss has the potential for leading to depression, physical illness, and heavy use of alcohol and illegal drugs, (Dohrenwend and Dohrenwend, 1974). Because work is so central to people's lives, the loss of a job is potentially very stressful, particularly if it is the result of massive, involuntary, permanent unemployment, as it was with the decline of Pittsburgh's heavy industry. The collapse of the region's manufacturing economy left many feeling uncertain and helpless about the future. Research has found that the impact from job loss can be eased or buffered by having access to other people, particularly family and friends, who are empathetic, understanding, and supportive. The impact can also be reduced by adaptive coping skills which enable a person to focus on the problem rather than on one's self (Liem and Rayman, 1982).

SOCIAL SUPPORT

The overwhelming majority of these fathers (83 percent) reported having at least one confidant to whom they could turn in a time of need while a smaller percentage (17 percent) reported having no one. When fathers who had experienced major job loss (MJL) were compared with those who had not, little difference was found between the two groups; that is, the support patterns for men who experienced MJL were virtually indistinguishable from those who had not. When comparing the fathers with their partners, it was found that slightly more of the partners (96 percent compared to 86 percent of the fathers) reported having contact every day or several times a week, while in the matched group, 41 percent of the fathers and 54 percent of their partners reported having daily or weekly contact with a support resource. Interestingly, 14 percent of all fathers reporting having access to support indicated having contact less than once a month. In the matched group, 13 percent of the fathers and 5 percent of their partners indicated having contact less than once a month.

Sixty-three percent of all of the fathers had someone to whom they could turn whereas 84 percent of the matched fathers and 84 percent of their partners had someone. When worried about their jobs, 70 percent of all fathers and 66 percent of their partners had someone to whom they could turn. Women reported having slightly greater access to support for particular types of problems than their partners.

Overall, neither the fathers nor their wives reported excessive depression. However, the wives' reported slightly higher levels of depressive symptoms than either group of fathers. Having more symptoms is consistent with other research that shows a correlation between gender and depression i.e., women, in general, tend to be more depressive than men (Radloff, 1977). Further, there was only a slight difference between fathers who had suffered major job loss and those who had not, with the latter slightly less likely to have symptoms. No relationship was found between current unemployment and depression. By itself, job loss did not appear to be highly correlated with depression and its symptoms.

When the relationship between depressive symptoms and social support was examined, little evidence was found that the two were related. That is, fathers who had less extensive supports did not report more depressive symptoms. This relationship was also examined by focusing on whether the support came from a spouse for the matched group of fathers and their wives. These results reveal that, among the fathers in the matched group of 101, the relationship between depressive symptomatology and spousal support is very weak, but among the wives the relationship is significant. The finding again lends support to the importance of gender in understanding depression.

It seemed to the researchers that the relationship between depression and being able to count on one's spouse for support could have implications for the quality of the marital relationship. And, at least among these wives and mothers, the hunch proved correct. There appears to be a very strong relationship between depressive symptomatology and marital satisfaction, however, for the matched fathers the relationship, is weaker than the one for wives. Overall, fathers were more satisfied with their marriages than wives, but this is not surprising since research has consistently shown that in every marriage there are actually two marriages; a his marriage and a her marriage.

Drinking is another maladaptive, but common, strategy for coping with stress. To explore this, data were obtained on current and past drinking habits. The questions about current drinking habits reveal that 80 percent of the complete sample of 516 fathers drank while 20 percent did not. In the matched group of 101 couples, 24 percent of the fathers and 41 percent of their partners reported not drinking at all. Beer is the drink of choice for all groups. There was a difference between the fathers and their wives. Approximately a fifth of the fathers indicated that they drank ten drinks or more on occasions.

RESEARCH FINDINGS

Major Job Loss

The consequences of fathers of young children having sustained a major job loss were of particular interest in this study. As can be seen in the preceding pages, there were both personal and family consequences. These are compounded by the community-wide consequences when tens of thousands of wage earners lose the source of their financial stability in a short period of time. But while there was suffering and personal tragedy, there appears to have been powerful and widespread resilience. Fathers who experienced major job loss do not appear very different now from the fathers who did not have a major job loss. The evidence suggests strong coping skills but, to some extent, a pattern of compensating for losses which may be less than ideal for their families. Indeed, many children and partners experienced the job loss very directly and paid a heavy price for it.

One of the more encouraging and hopeful findings is that these fathers and families are in rather good health. The fathers themselves showed little evidence of physical health problems or symptoms associated with depression. They have stable marriages and, to a significant extent, supportive extended families upon whom they can rely for assistance in child care and other needs.

Current Economic Situation

Even when combining the data for all 516 randomly selected fathers in this study, their situation in the 1990s is alarming. The extent of unemployment, underemployment, loss of income, and other indicators of personal, family, and community well-being are foreboding and point toward some problems not likely to be remedied quickly-even with substantial improvements in the regional economy.

Since the samples were drawn from communities in which a third or more of workers were employed in manufacturing industries in 1980, it is not surprising that the sample was a predominantly working-class group. Nor is it surprising that this group was hit hard by the economic forces which shaped the 1980s. What is noteworthy is the extent to which their economic situation continues to languish years after the collapse.

Unemployment continues at a crisis rate of 8.9 percent. An additional 8.5 percent have been able to find only part-time employment. Thus, nearly one-fifth (17.4 percent) of the fathers either had no employment or were underemployed in the 1990s. Indeed, 13 percent of all fathers reported incomes below the poverty level, 19.4 percent reported less income than five years ago and 11.7 percent had no health insurance. To help cope with this, more than half of the fathers' partners (56 percent) were employed, 27 percent of them full-time. And, as pointed out, the situation for non-white families is most alarming, with one-half having poverty incomes below $1,000 per month. For many of these, family income is far below $1,000. Home ownership for non-white fathers was also substantially beneath the level for white fathers.

What emerges is a rather unpleasant picture of working families entering the 1990s with continuing widespread economic distress resulting from both recent events and long-standing social and economic factors.

The effects were extensive and reached into every facet of life. Recovery is a long way off for many of these fathers and their families. Whatever the reasons, a sizable group remains in grave straits. These are not chronically unemployed men of the kind who are frequently characterized as unemployable. Indeed, the interviews did not disclose a single father who was not employed at some time during the eight-year period studied.

It is impossible to escape the serious implications of these conditions for children and families. One important group of concerns involves education and job training.

Education and Training

There appears to be a group of men with vocational training for whom suitable jobs do not exist. This stable, healthy, rooted and well educated (both vocationally and in terms of higher education) population should be readily employable. The slow growth in the economy, the modest increase in available technical jobs for which workers might be retrained and the more rapid growth in the number of low paying, often service-related jobs, do not bode well for the economic future of this group. Given the mean age of 35 years for this sample, one might say that the average unemployed or underemployed father is faced with as many as thirty years in an uninviting labor market. He is trained for jobs that do not exist; he can expect low wages for the jobs that do exist; the training programs that might be devised to prepare workers for sophisticated jobs in high technology firms are not numerous and may never be. This generation of fathers will grow older, subject to economic stress and frustration. Under such conditions, it is particularly difficult for fathers who were previously accustomed to providing for their families in an adequate fashion to remain effective role models.

Fathers and Their Families

It is discouraging to verify what other studies have indicated—that fathers remain relatively uninvolved in child care responsibilities, continuing to leave most child rearing to their wives. Fathers tend to see their child caretaking role as limited largely to play, leaving nurturing and day-to-day tasks to their partners. What especially typifies the group examined here is the relative homogeneity of both their behavior and attitudes. There are few fathers who break the pattern. Moreover, most of the fathers are comfortable with this level of engagement with their children; few show any interest in egalitarian child caretaking for their families.

While increased time at home appears to enlarge a father's child care involvement, it appears to do so only temporarily. Greater experience with child rearing does not create the desire in fathers to maintain such involvement. Major job loss fathers reported that immediately after they lost their jobs, they took on more responsibility for child care. However, today, they are not more engaged with their children than other fathers, and their beliefs about the extent to which they should be involved are as conservative as those of fathers who did not lose their jobs. Likewise, fathers who are now unemployed report doing more child care, but their beliefs about how child caretaking should be divided in the family remain traditional.

A finding of great concern to us is the relatively large group of fathers (at least one in five) who give evidence of difficulty in attaching to their children. An even larger group of fathers (one in four) believes their youngest children are not responsive to them, suggesting these fathers do not find interaction with their young children very pleasurable. The findings also suggest that fathers sometimes blame their children for their sense of social distance, feeling it is because the children cannot respond to them and that they, in turn, are unattached. Because attachment capabilities are considered a crucial cornerstone of healthy child development (Erikson, 1994), this finding raises questions about the effects of such distant parental styles on the growing child. Do these children grow up believing that men are not easy to relate to, that fathers are not people to whom one turns for nurturance?

Our finding that the extent of a father's satisfaction with his marriage is associated with the level of his satisfaction with parenting is an important one, in that it points to families who are in double jeopardy. Fathers whose marriages are less satisfactory do not compensate for these feelings by becoming closer to their children. Instead, they tend to feel less attached to them, and to state that child caretaking places more restrictions on them. Fathers who find themselves in unhappy marital situations may, then, be particularly prone to disengaging from their children.

The special plight of fathers who are working multiple jobs needs to be considered as well. For these fathers, there is relatively less involvement in child care across the entire spectrum of parental activities. They not only do fewer daily child care tasks; they also play less with their children. When these fathers find themselves burdened with additional stress, emotional or physical, they also tend to become less attached to their children. At the same time, they tend to feel that their children are less responsive to them. Fathers who are relieved of these heavy work demands do not disassociate themselves from their children to the same degree as when faced with other severe stresses.

Child Care

The fathers interviewed for the study show a strong preference for providing child care within their immediate or extended family. Child care is provided by partners, fathers, relatives, and friends in that order. Very limited use of paid day care was noted. Families are seen as the best place for child rearing. Nevertheless, as indicated above, the fathers' perceptions of their roles are quite traditional and rather limited in scope.

In addition, partners-to whom the heaviest child caring responsibilities fall-are often employed outside the home and carry a disproportionate share of household responsibilities. Providing child care is especially problematic when both parents work the same shift. In more than half of the families in which both the fathers and their partners were employed, both parents were out of the home at the same time. Even more important, nearly one-third of both the fathers and their partners were away working after 6:00 p.m. Child care is critical for children during this time when meals, homework, play time, personal care, and bed time must be provided by caretakers other than the parents. In nearly as many families, both parents were absent from home because of work during the daytime hours. For families with pre-school children who prefer family child care to day care, this amounts to a sizeable demand on extended family members.

POLICY IMPLICATIONS OF THE EFFECTS
OF ECONOMIC RESTRUCTURING FOR FAMILIES

In all fairness, it must be observed that while a substantial minority of these fathers face severe difficulties now or in the future, the majority of fathers interviewed for this study and their families have adapted satisfactorily. Their incomes are higher than five years ago; marriages, jobs, rates of home ownership, and health, for example, suggest normally satisfying life styles. At the same time they live in communities where depleted tax bases have undermined such things as public schools, public safety, and other public services for all residents regardless of whether they are among those who suffered job loss. All were adversely affected, to some extent, by the demise of manufacturing in the area. Therefore, it should not be assumed that the recommendations to follow are directed only toward the needs of those immediately affected by major job loss.

Public awareness and public acknowledgement of the continuing, long-term serious consequences of the economic changes of the last decade must be evoked. For a variety of political, personal, and other reasons there has been widespread public and private inattention to many of these problems. Some were once concerned but have tired or believe the problems have been remedied. Others choose routinely to ignore and deny the extent of human need in their communities. Still others fear admission of the problems will require costly solutions they would prefer not to finance. Some have been influenced by reports that the economic conditions in the area have improved, and promises of a bright employment future for the Pittsburgh area. Despite these rosy assessments and predictions, the evidence from this study suggests unemployment and underemployment are lingering problems and not likely to disappear in the foreseeable future. The jobs that were lost were steady, full-time, well-paid jobs and have not been replaced. The typical response to the loss of these jobs has been serial employment, a shift to a two-income family, or lowering the standard of living. Public apathy or self-serving denial of human need are age-old problems and not likely to disappear either, but in the absense of awareness, nothing will move public officials, business, leaders, citizens groups, religious bodies, private social service agencies, school districts, and others able to improve conditions.

A wide range of educational opportunities including job training must be made available for the victims of the economic dislocation that has racked the region. This is not to minimize the vocational educational training and retraining and related programs already offered by a variety of sponsors in the region. But the number of opportunities is well-known to be inadequate, as is the need for family financial support during periods of training, especially for the poor. Coordination of job training and realistic future job opportunities are also insufficient.

The field of vocational education is not an area of special expertise of the present authors and was not the focus of this study. However, one cannot avoid underscoring the findings of others that there is an enormous gap between the needs of the unemployed and future employment opportunities. Programs that may exist certainly have not reached the fathers we interviewed.

Traditional Gender-Role Beliefs Constrain Adaptation to economic change. A heavy burden was laid upon the partners and children of this Pittsburgh area sample of fathers as a consequence of combined economic problems and a traditional division of labor. Partners often must seek employment, provide emotional support, and carry heavy household and child-rearing responsibilities. And, sadly, fathers are content with this. Children may be denied the attachment bonds with their fathers necessary for full, normal, healthy development. Partners must seek employment when their responsibilities are already heavy. And again, unfortunately, fathers seem content with this.

Employers, public policy makers, educators, job training and job development professionals, health care providers, the courts, families, and others share the imperative to address gender inequality.

Nontraditional programs and methods must be devised to serve fathers, especially young fathers, in our society. In a time when human services are being successfully developed to meet the needs of the elderly and a wide range of other special populations, it should not be difficult to devise creative, attractive and helpful programs to meet the needs of fathers. Many existing social services are staffed largely by women and have been designed historically on the premise that women and mothers are the family members primarily responsible for the nurturance of children and the functioning of their families. Many of the services welcome families and many serve them well. Certainly there is no reason not to have services for women and mothers. But it is clear that many fathers lack opportunities to learn better ways of relating to their children and gaining a balanced view of their role as fathers.

One possible explanation for the relative health and well-being of the fathers studied, as reported earlier, is that they have and avail themselves of a range of informal supports. Because they already use outside supports, it should be possible for more formalized services to reach and engage them.

Public and private human service agencies, employee assistance programs, professional schools preparing a range of practitioners serving families, religious organizations, and others can help. This may be one of the special opportunities for the churches to whom these fathers expressed attachment to become involved.

The depressive quality of life in Pittsburgh's barren "mill towns" must be addressed. This is a classic example of one area in which all families are affected. Economic woes drive municipalities and school districts to discard all but the most essential services. Playgrounds, recreational programs and facilities, special family events, concerts, children's theater, and countless similar programs are set aside in favor of paying the electric bill for the traffic signals.

Help for families and children to escape television as a primary form of recreation is limited in general but is even more scant in the local communities where the families interviewed in this study are strongly rooted. When physical and cultural surroundings are drab, strong measures are needed to help families and children see beyond the confines of their immediate situation.

County and state governments, foundations, corporations and a variety of private organizations must take these needs seriously if recovery and local self-sufficiency in this area are ever to be restored.

Economic supports for families must be strengthened. The limitations on general assistance in Pennsylvania, the appalling inadequacy of health care for poor and working poor families, the inability of many families to take advantage of educational and training opportunities because of inadequate family financial supports, and the large number of children not served by nutritional supplement programs are but a few examples of the problem. While there is no substitute for employment with a livable income, it is evident this is not always going to happen. Children are often prime victims when economic troubles strike. Society must eventually foot the bill for the consequences of such problems as inadequate nutrition and health care, and the lifetime costs are staggering.

Federal and state governments must provide the resources to meet these needs, but all citizens must provide the pressures that lead to public action.

Child care that meets the needs of a wide range of families must be provided. Highly visible on the agendas or both political parties, a wide range of professional organizations and, not least, many families, is child care. Sometimes referred to as day care, it is one of the commonly accepted needs in our society although consensus on the means to meet this need has not been reached. Day care is in high demand, yet parents often cannot afford the cost or do not trust the circumstances in which such care is offered.

The fathers and families described here have a very limited interest in paid, professional day care, preferring instead to rely on an extended family and neighborhood network. What these families may need most are short-term day care opportunities for infrequent or irregular usage and a variety of other options and supports that reinforce their family orientation. There is a need for a functional, supportive system of assuring the safety and well-being of the vast numbers of children cared for in the communities where families live. Were more fathers and mothers drawn into some of the new, nontraditional services for families, e.g., neighborhood child care centers staffed with people from the same communities, this informal or "shadow child care system" might relieve some of the stress placed on these families who are working around the clock. As we reported earlier in this chapter, many of the fathers worked long hours and sometimes neither parent was available at home during the early evening hours when children need special care and attention. This situation is very hard on families and could well be detrimental to children's well-being. The findings from our research clearly show that there is a high demand for new, nontraditional childcare services.

Chapter 12

The Needs and Concerns
of Youth in a Depressed Area:
A Brief Report

Lambert Maguire
Hide Yamatani

Pittsburgh's economic downturn was particularly harmful to local youth. Among their traditional doors to opportunity, one (the mill) closed permanently and the other two (college and the military) began restricting entrance as resources diminished. Between 1981 and 1986, the unemployment rate for Pittsburgh youths aged 16 to 21 exceeded 21 percent (Pennsylvania Department of Labor, cited in Faughan et al., 1987). In the midst of downspiralling economic change, young people have to reconsider their futures. This pilot project set out specifically to discover what choices young people were making in response to economic change and the accompanying stress.

The sample was composed of young people from several sites in the Pittsburgh area and in the region surrounding Dublin, Ireland. Only the American sample and the findings emanating from interviews with American youth are discussed here. These young people were not randomly selected from the youth populations available. Rather, the sample was purposive and designed to obtain young people from economically isolated areas with high unemployment rates. Eighty-three were surveyed in a high school in a distressed steel town in the Monongahela Valley. The questionnaire was given to all eleventh and twelfth graders in English classes. Another four young people were interviewed in Monessen High School, bringing the total from Monessen to 87. The remainder of the sample was recruited from two training programs in and around the Pittsburgh area.

These young people were not expected to have completed the transition from school to work, that is, to be full-fledged members of the workforce. Rather, they were viewed as average youth facing uncertain times, and probably affected by the unemployment experiences of family and friends. The total sample size in the United States was 119. The group was racially mixed with 29 percent black, 66.7 percent white, and 4.3 percent other, and almost evenly divided along gender lines with 49.2 percent male and 50.8 percent female. A questionnaire made up of 31 items related to educational and work experience, household social and economic data, and experiences with seeking support or assistance in times of stress was used. Included in the questionnaire were standardized measures of depression, self-esteem, and social support.

THE PROBLEMS YOUTH FACE

In spite of their youthfulness and student status, many of these young people wanted to be in the workforce in some capacity. As noted in the women and household unemployment study, one reason for this may be to try to alleviate economic hardship at home. Approximately one-third (31 percent) were working part-time at the time of the study. A similar proportion (32 percent) desired part-time work, and a small number (7 percent) wanted full-time work. Thirty-six percent or 43 of the Americans reported they were not working because there were "no jobs," while 19 percent were unemployed by choice. Only 3 percent believed that a lack of skills on their part was the reason for their unemployment. They perceived problems with transportation as a more significant barrier to obtaining employment (13 percent).

The young people were, by and large, willing to leave town to search for work in the future. Seventy-three percent, evenly divided by gender, indicated their willingness to leave. These findings are compatible with those of a 1986 survey done in the mill town of Duquesne in the Monongahela Valley that found that those leaving the community to work elsewhere tended to be young (Biegel et al., 1989). Another survey, conducted by the *Pittsburgh Post-Gazette,* found that 60 percent of high school residents from seven mill town school districts were planning to leave their hometowns to seek employment elsewhere (Blotzer, 1986). What of true emigration? When asked if they were willing to leave the United States, 18.6 percent of this sample said "yes" while another 44 percent said "maybe." These responses suggest that the future outpouring of youth from the Pittsburgh area, even if only to neighboring states, may be quite significant and have dramatic consequences.

As anticipated by the investigators, these young people were experiencing some social/ psychological difficulties. They were asked to indicate if any of the following had been problems for them personally in the past three years: (a) feelings of depression, nervousness, or anxiety; (b) drinking and drugs (including street drugs); (c) increased family arguments and fights; and (d) other emotional problems. Family arguments and fights was checked most often (36 percent), with almost half of the females indicating that this was a problem for them. Depression, nervousness, or anxiety affected 32 percent, and drinking and drugs were checked by 13 percent. As a check on the very subjective nature of the question about experiencing problems with depression, nervousness, or anxiety, this item was run against overall scores from a validated depression scale, the Zung Self-Rating Depression Scale (SDS) (in Corcoran and Fischer, 1987) . There was good correspondence in that those reporting that they had problems in the previous three years also had higher scores on the scale, i.e., more reported symptoms of depression.

Asked about specific types of other emotional problems that they had faced, the young people who responded were almost evenly divided between boyfriend/girlfriend problems (12 percent) and money/jobs/unemployment (11 percent). SDS scores for depression, though they indicated that a small proportion of youths were having problems, did not indicate extensive clinical problems among these young people. As described below, they reported for the most part positive feelings about the support available to them from family and friends.

WHERE THEY GO FOR HELP

Friends, neighbors, and relatives were singled out as the sources of support these young people relied upon most for help. Most were satisfied with the help they received from these informal supports. All respondents relying on friends and neighbors, for example, indicated that they found those persons to be either "very willing" to help (65 percent) or "willing" to help (35 percent). Those relying most on relatives similarly reported that most were "very willing" (57 percent) or at least "willing" (33 percent) to help. Only a few respondents (9.5 percent) indicated that relatives were "not very willing" to help. Equal proportions found the help that they received "very satisfying" (33 percent of those relying upon relatives and 35 percent of those relying upon friends and neighbors) or "satisfying" (62 percent of those seeking support from relatives and 65 percent of those seeking support from friends and neighbors). Only one young person, relying most upon relatives, checked "very dissatisfied" in response to the question.

These findings supported those emanating from studies of adults in the region, as reported in Part Four. The sources of support considered informal or natural—friends, neighbors, relatives—were consistently called upon to help when people felt they needed help. The investigators, looking at the situation of these young people and the difficult times ahead for them as they sought entry into a markedly flattened economy, saw a need to build broader networks of support for these young people generally. One suggestion was to find ways of linking the formal supports (training, income maintenance, health care, and the like that might be needed later) to the informal supports the young people already utilized.

The projects developed for youth described in Part Five pick up on some of these themes. With little being done to assist young people in this region, local community groups began efforts to simultaneously build alternative opportunity structures for youth, to link them to the workforce, and to broaden their local networks of support.

SUMMARY

Across the action research in Parts Three and Four, first using the community as the unit of analysis, and later examining household types and special populations, a body of evidence about the mill towns was compiled. The findings were shared in a preliminary and informal way with communities that requested feedback from the school. Later on, the more formal River Community Project Seminar Series would be held at the University of Pittsburgh to provide more complete and detailed analysis. For the Seminar Series, not only would the research findings be available, but assessments of community organization and demonstration projects would be topics for presentation and discussion. For initial purposes, however, going out to the towns upon request was often a faster and more convenient arrangement for the residents, and the reports given by researchers also generated useful discussion on local projects or prospective local projects.

Trips to the communities served several purposes. The Aliquippa Alliance, for example, organized a local mini-conference focusing on results from the longitudinal study and the women's study. In other places, there were press conferences in the communities with school faculty and students as participants. One was held in East Liberty when the Youth Enterprise Projects were awarded funds; another was held in Monessen to celebrate the opening of the Youth Enterprise Demonstration Project headquarters on the main street of the town and the simultaneous opening of two small businesses.

The messages from the River Community Project's research findings were presented at the mini-conferences and press conferences. They are summarized below as a fitting ending to Part Four. The messages provide the basic materials to move to Part Five, where community organization and demonstration projects are the focus of attention. The summary begins with a synopsis of events in the river communities just prior to the initiation of the River Communities Project. It continues with results from the research in two parts. The first chronicles the damage done to the communities; the second describes the impact on households and families.

In the early 1980s, most of the mills in the river communities around Pittsburgh closed or moved away. The people living in southwestern Pennsylvania were accustomed to market swings that produced periodic layoffs, but the mills and the good jobs had always come back. This time it was different. The stunned population had to realize that the layoffs were permanent. In Part Three, action research carefully documented the extent and persistence of the economic devastation following the departure of the mills. In Part Four a more formal series of action research projects was launched, focusing on specific goals and targets identified in the exploratory phase. The findings are presented in brief form below.

First, the damage done in this region:

1. Five, six, and even seven years later, studies showed that the mill towns of southwestern Pennsylvania had not recovered from the very severe decline in opportunities for employment that descended on their communities in the early 1980s. Most of the well-paying jobs were gone, Main Street shops were boarded up, young people were moving away to find better work opportunities, and the population was shrinking and aging. The tax base for municipal services was also sharply declining, leaving school programs deteriorating and crime rates rising.

2. The mill towns and the people who lived there were besieged from every side. Jobs were scarce and inadequate. What jobs there were were less and less likely to offer retirement pensions or health benefits. Managing health care became a major problem in the river towns.

3. People lost their homes or had to move to less expensive, less desirable housing. There was no money for repairs or for replacements of worn-out stoves, refrigerators, and other appliances in the homes people did have. Some respondents reported having to resort to the dreaded public assistance. It was a downward spiral for workers who for generations had lived in towns where workers were rewarded for their skills, and who anticipated that their children and their children's children would be able to stay on in the region. The worst part of the spiral was that it showed no signs of turning upward.

4. The desperate situation of the mill towns went largely unheeded. There was very little public financial support available to the small, often quite isolated mill towns. In fact, the mill towns tended to be ignored. The new Republican administration in Washington did not respond to requests for help to alleviate the disaster. The state gave small amounts here and

there, and most of that after the severe deterioration of the communities and their infrastructures had made them wastelands. Local governments also responded tardily, being at first most concerned with more populous areas. Later local governments became strapped for funds and called on the private sector to help. By this time the private sector too was becoming exhausted by the mounting appeals for their limited funds. Advocates for the rescue of the mill towns, both individual and group, did not have much influence, given the forces arrayed against them.

Second, the resources needed at the individual, family, or household level:

1. Across all of the action research, good jobs were the priority craving everywhere. These were not unemployable people, but people with good employment records and education and skills. They continuously sought work and also additional education and training to get work. Their training needs were largely ignored; the inadequate opportunities available were often allocated to the already employed. For other needs such as support, financial assistance, child care, and a myriad of everyday needs, the residents in the river communities turned to informal social supports, especially family and friends. It was to these supports that they turned in desperate times and, by all accounts, their supports responded. Even though family members were suffering their own deprivations and sorrows, they could always be counted on.

2. Formal supports from agencies and organizations were less prominently mentioned. The respondents were religiously oriented for the most part, and the church was a natural source of comfort and, to a lesser extent, material support. Only in the six-community study and the women's study do we get extended, specific questions about formal support. Taking this together with what is available in the other action research, it is evident that reliance on formal support systems is not very strong in the isolated, often ethnically oriented communities. It is clear that many respondents needed more medical attention than they were able to procure, but it is also clear that they

were not always satisfied with the medical care they did receive. Help from mental health agencies through counseling was sought in some instances and provided some relief, but again disappointment with assistance received was high, much higher than for medical services. The women, it was discovered, expressed satisfaction with the formal services they received, although some complained about going from place to place to obtain a minimum amount of the necessities of life. The women traipsed around endlessly to obtain enough food, shelter, and energy supplies to fulfill the basic needs of their families.

3. All information collected suggested strongly that informal supports were the main sources of help and that the respondents were most satisfied with informal support. But were these usually small networks, often themselves needing help, enough? Women, for example, expressed utmost satisfaction with their at least one and usually two confidants. But when asked what was most needed from the community, the first priority for this sample was "more support groups." The fathers wanted to keep child care "all in the family," but it was evident that managing this responsibility was causing conflict between parents, and resentment on the part of both fathers and mothers. Unemployed children could rely on elderly parents and, indeed, considerable support was forthcoming, but at least in some cases those parents suffered deprivation themselves in order to help their children and their grandchildren. There is some evidence that physical and mental health professionals tried to be responsive, but they did not always reach people who surely could have used their services. Some of this is undoubtedly due to resistance on the part of members of these communities, but some is probably due to lack of rapid, targeted response to the needs of individuals and families caught up in disaster.

PART FIVE:
RESEARCH AND DEMONSTRATION:
PUTTING FINDINGS INTO ACTION

A key element in the River Communities Project was to provide direct, targeted support to community self-help groups. Action-oriented research was intended to supply an information base on which social action could be planned more effectively. The mini-conferences in which the results from the first two phases were presented, as described at the end of Part Four, were intended to stimulate community projects. In fact, by the time research results were being discussed with community leaders and residents and with the School's graduate students in community organization, plans had begun to germinate. The exploratory phase of the research had hardly begun when the River Communities Project began to give support to fledgling community organization projects. The need for promoting community unity and cooperation had become very apparent from the exploratory research.

The first chapter in Part Five, Chapter 13, describes several community organization projects that were initiated in the exploratory phase. This is only a small slice of the many self-help efforts mounted in the mill towns. The River Communities Project was involved with more than a dozen different community self-help groups at one time or another. The ones described in Chapter 13 were chosen because they are the ones we know most about. Carefully compiled documentation of the activities engaged in, the successes and setbacks, was kept on these projects. In retrospect, it became clear that these records took us deeper into mill town experiences than research could manage to penetrate. Self-help projects revealed the intensity of the struggle to build communities when the social fabric of neighborhood relationships, organizations, institutions, and leadership had been grossly undermined if not damaged beyond repair. The barriers created by the destruction were formidable; it took enormous patience and dedicated people who were in it for the long haul to move toward tackling the endless problems, problems that fed upon one another.

Early community organization efforts were sometimes sustained long enough to spill over into the second phase of the project in the form of demonstration projects. The projects described in Chapter 14 also derived some impetus from the exploratory action research, since commentary on "vanishing youth" was a major theme in every locale. Youth departure in search of better opportunities elsewhere seemed to be accepted with regret mingled with fatalism. It seemed clear, however, that the departure of a large segment of the youth of the region would damage the opportunities for renewal. The research from Chapter 12 on needs and concerns of youth in a depressed area demonstrated that fears about losing the vitality of young people were well grounded. Most of the young people interviewed were seriously thinking of moving elsewhere to find work. Little action had been taken to attempt to retain youth in the mill towns, although in one of the community organization projects to be discussed, activities had spread to include pilot programs with young people, and other communities were at least considering moves in that direction.

Eventually three youth enterprise projects were initiated in three different communities, as described in Chapter 14. The school helped with project designs and planning in conjunction with interested community groups and leaders. Faculty researchers agreed to conduct evaluations of the three demonstration projects in order to obtain substantial financial assistance from the Appalachian Regional Commission. Evaluating the demonstrations also provided new insights into the communities, as the demonstrations were concrete examples of the depth of the struggle to get anything—even something everyone seemed to advocate—to become a going concern.

The last chapter in Part Five describes the River Communities Project Seminar Series. Several mini-conferences provided opportunities to offer rapid feedback to mill towns about research results and to discuss possible community projects in strategic locations in an informal way. What was reported on and discussed was recounted in the last part of Part Four. The seminars were a more formal device for sharing with interested community members, colleagues, professionals, and politicians in the Pittsburgh area the results of the overall efforts. The press was also encouraged to come, in part to secure the maximum dissemination of the findings. The seminars are briefly reported on, for they provide an important bridge to the more contemplative final project phase, Part Six, in which a critical review of the project is coupled with consideration of emergent themes in micro level policy. That discussion in turn leads to defining the limits of grassroots policy efforts without significant assistance from the state and/or federal government when economic catastrophe occurs.

Chapter 13

Selected
Community Organization
Efforts

Field placements are a required and major part of the curriculum for students at the University of Pittsburgh School of Social Work. A survey carried out in late 1989 with master's and undergraduate students showed that the great majority thought of the field placement as a priority part, if not *the* priority part, of the educational process (Baum, 1989). The community organization curriculum each year attracts a number of students who not only look forward to their field placements but also sometimes seek out their own opportunities. The River Communities Project benefited from student efforts to develop unique placements and to write formal reports on what they learned in the process of trying to build new organizations.

Cathy Cairns utilized the placement requirement to begin the work necessary to develop the Aliquippa Alliance for Unity and Development (AAUD). Professor James Cunningham served as her advisor and encouraged her to write up her experiences in building this organization for a report titled *Aliquippa Update: A Pittsburgh Milltown Struggles to Come Back, 1984-86* (Cairns and Cunningham, 1986).

In another river valley outside of Pittsburgh, two other community-organizing master's students, Matthew Hawkins and Mike Eichler, worked on a project to develop a local credit union, the Homestead Community Credit Union. Matt Hawkins was encouraged to develop a paper on the experience, and both Cairns and Hawkins were encouraged to submit their papers for inclusion in the bound report *Steel People*. Part of the significance of including the two community organization papers, along with research reports, was symbolic. The River Communities Project was interested not only in documenting the decline of the region's mill towns and related communities but also intended to actively engage in developing new organizations and institutions through demonstration projects. The work of students such as Hawkins, Eichler, and Cairns provided important insights on the how-tos of working in these communities, knowledge that could be used in classes on strategies and tactics in organizing, and that could be used to build future demonstration projects in distressed communities.

THE ALIQUIPPA ALLIANCE

Cathy Cairns appropriately titled her submission to the report *Aliquippa Update* "The Aliquippa Alliance for Unity and Development: An Organizer's Perspective of the Initial Effort." It should prove fascinating to students interested in community organizing in that it has much to say about how such work can begin and about the level of commitment required from someone interested in such work. All of the detail Cairns incorporated cannot be included here. Rather, the focus of what follows is upon the links between her work in the community and the project developed by the School, and how such efforts could be carried out elsewhere in similar situations.

The activities leading up to the development of the Aliquippa Alliance could be said to characterize a community-organizing effort that is simultaneously goal-directed and process-oriented. They also represent organizing that is community- or place-grounded rather than issue-oriented. The parties involved had an overarching goal related to place prosperity, that is, to concretely helping residents and changing the course of Aliquippa's decline. With that as their mission, participants focused upon the community's needs, and the actual direction of their work unfolded as information was gathered. An initial concern for the plight of the unemployed in Aliquippa, for example, led to interest in the establishment of a local unemployed committee (Cairns, 1986). Unemployed committees developed in a number of communities in southwestern Pennsylvania and were organized on a regional basis as a vehicle of self-help for the unemployed. The committees provided hot-line services and advocacy for unemployed people and their families (River Communities Project, 1989).

From the beginning Cathy Cairns was joined in the community organization process by Lorenzo Williams, then Vice President of the National Association for the Advancement of Colored People (NAACP) in Aliquippa. In the process of organizing support for the unemployed committee, the organizers learned about other things that needed attention. After discussing plans with local unemployed residents and community leaders, both Williams and Cairns decided that Aliquippa's problems needed more than an effort focused on organizing the unemployed. "The initial core group wanted more than the empowerment of the unemployed from a major effort–they wanted action that could impact the conditions in the town, the causes of unemployment, creation of jobs, and attraction of social services to the area" (Cairns, 1986, p. 67).

From this point on, the work in Aliquippa related very much to the findings of the original Aliquippa study. Continued fieldwork by key activists produced a list of local individuals (residents and community leaders) to invite to an initial organizing meeting of the AAUD. The invitees were broadly representative of the community, including leaders of opposing political factions; key figures from the steelworkers' local, the NAACP, local businesses, and churches; and other community residents. They represented the resources identified as "keys in a recovery effort" in the conclusion of the original Aliquippa study (Blocher et al., 1984).

The work proceeded to identify the most critical problems facing the community and how they might be addressed collectively. Process became critical to the birth of the Alliance. Developing an organization broadly representative of the community meant bringing together diverse parties to forge agreements and commitments that could be sustained. The initiating group had to come to a consensus on a philosophy and a mission for the organization and how both could be formalized. Everything about the Aliquippa Alliance was drawn in a comprehensive framework. Those who developed the organization wanted to address the needs of community residents (retraining the unemployed), the problems facing the town (from racial tension to lack of unified leadership), and business development (Cairns, 1986, p. 69).

The group subsequently began providing human services at a local level, conducting an inventory of available property in the local business district, and developing events to enhance pride in the community. Relations between the police and the community also became a focus. The resulting organization could be characterized as a "hybrid" (Ahlbrandt and Cunningham, 1979), utilizing pressure to achieve goals and simultaneously providing direct services. The description of the birth and initial work of the Alliance, published in *Aliquippa Update* (Cairns and Cunningham, 1986), concluded with a note of uncertainty. Cairns noted that, while growing in strength, the AAUD had not yet made use of that strength to pressure critical resources, such as county government and the owner of the LTV Steel mill site. Subsequent material, however, shows that the Aliquippa Alliance continued its rapid growth and is now firmly established in the community. The scope and reach of its activities approximate those of a local government.

In January 1994, Pauline Cooper became the executive director of the Alliance, following the resignation of Cathy Cairns. No stranger to Aliquippa or the mill towns, Pauline, while an MSW student at the University of Pittsburgh, had interviewed local leaders in Aliquippa for the report *Aliquippa Update*. Upon graduation, she worked for six and a half years as a community organizer for the Mon Valley Initiative, a community development organization (more about the Initiative later in this chapter). She worked to develop community development corporations and foster economic development in some of the Mon Valley's poorest mill towns, including Braddock and Clairton.

The Alliance continues to follow its principal mission under her direction, pursuing broad efforts to improve life in Aliquippa. Partnerships are being forged with the local school district and Robert Morris College, to improve the quality of local education. Youth employment and training programs continue. Local beautification projects have begun, as well, that capitalize upon the talents of professional artists and enhance the cultural life of the community. Further attention is given to Aliquippa in Part Six.

The course of action followed by the organizers of the Alliance confirmed and strengthened the mission of the River Communities Project. The initial field study of the community helped to identify elements and local leadership critical to building a broadly representative community-based institution. Action-oriented research, it was confirmed, could aid in the planned implementation of social change. The support was mutual. The continued work of the Alliance aided the River Communities Project in later years, as the enduring relationship provided direction for future research and demonstration efforts. For example, the Alliance took on the development of broad-based youth employment and training programs. The knowledge gained by working with youth in that community made more credible, concrete, and realizable the River Communities Project's growing interest in demonstration initiatives related to youth opportunities.

In essence, a mutually beneficial relationship developed. Action-oriented research supported the birth of a new initiative committed to social change and aware of the value of continued research. The emerging organization, pursuing its own objectives, provided new information on community needs, supporting future research, demonstration initiatives, and joint ventures involving the River Communities Project. This is not to say that, at every step of the way, the relationship between the project and the AAUD was always reassuring, supportive, or conflict free. University-based research can be viewed as exploitative of communities; residents may become hostile if they sense that their neighborhoods have become "laboratories" for ivory-tower professors. By the same token, universities may be fearful of being utilized as conduits for funding over which they have little control and through which they gain little benefit. There is always a great potential for misunderstanding and opposition between school and community.

It would be fair to state, however, that those involved in building the Alliance and the River Communities Project saw their relationship as more beneficial than harmful. Each brought resources to the other. Each endeavored to bring its own strengths to bear on the community's problems, sharing a commitment to improve the situation. Finding ways to build reciprocity is essential if school and community are to work well together.

THE HOMESTEAD COMMUNITY CREDIT UNION

The route taken in building the Homestead Community Credit Union was different from that followed in Aliquippa. Matt Hawkins and another master's student, Mike Eichler, came into the Homestead community as organizers with a specific mission: to build a community credit union. Both were advanced graduate students in the school's community organization program who were well informed about the distress in local communities. The goal from the outset in Homestead was to establish an organization to deliver a single service. Hawkins' report on the credit union and the organizing activity that generated it, published in the report *Steel People* (Cunningham and Martz, 1986), contains very similar organizing elements when compared with the "hybrid" AAUD in Aliquippa.

Homestead, like Aliquippa, was afflicted with political, social, and other fragmentation, latent and overt racial hostility, dramatic economic decline, and patterns of social disorganization. Although not as isolated as Aliquippa or as reliant upon a single dominant industry, Homestead was suffering and lacked united cooperative efforts to reverse the situation. It already had organizations concerned with its future and attempting to meet the human service needs of the unemployed. Although these entities were not as yet working well together, it seemed inadvisable to duplicate any ongoing local efforts.

Hawkins and Eichler did not involve the community in a broad-based effort to define its needs and develop an umbrella organization to take on community renewal. Rather, Homestead was approached as a community in which a number of key needs had already been identified. Some of the problems were already being addressed. A community credit union was a potential solution to a vital subset of problems not yet receiving attention. Specifically, work in Homestead was devoted to the problem of capital flight from a community undergoing rapid disinvestment. A community-based mechanism was needed for essential small projects, such as home and business improvements. The credit union, ideally, would move investment into the community and secure some community control over local investments. Successful organization of a credit union was also viewed as a strategy through which diverse people could unite the community in a positive effort, beneficial to all.

The initial organizing time was utilized to talk with local residents, businesspeople, and others about the relative merits of building a community credit union. This was, in essence, the initial test of the feasibility of the project. The organizers were aware from the outset that the concept would have relevance for many. Dramatic demonstrations had been targeted against specific banks in the area, most notably in Homestead, bringing negative publicity to the community. Because they were orchestrated to dramatize the role of the banks in disinvestment, the demonstrations probably encouraged some residents to invest in the credit union as a positive effort to stem capital flight. Community residents and businesspeople also were concerned with the deterioration of the local markets and the run-down appearance of the surrounding residential streets. A credit union could provide small loans for targeted improvements to homes and local businesses.

The project could not succeed, however, without sufficient active support at the local level. As in Aliquippa, the organizing strategy that was used relied heavily on the identification of local leadership. In this project a specific type of local leader was sought: people who were committed to action (as opposed to talk) and who represented divergent political views, but were not wedded to a particular approach to solving Homestead's problems. The organizers looked for what Fessler (1976) terms "expressive" leaders, those who see their own self-interest as best met through service to the community or group. Such people have specific, recognized capabilities, but may not be seen as "leaders." The known organizational and institutional heads, carrying the conferred status of "leadership," also had to be tapped as part of the process, but Hawkins' analysis of the building of the credit union pointed to the important role to be played by latent leadership.

The core group of committed local people necessarily had to be identified. The organizers did not have research already carried out in this particular community as a basis for this identification. Rather, they had to move about the community, get to know people as they talked about the credit union project, and make judgments about whom to involve. They utilized a specific strategy to gain symbolic individual commitments to the credit union. Pledge cards were developed. Those who signed the cards promised regular deposits with the credit union. As the pledge drive was begun, prospective members found out about others involved. This information was used to demonstrate the diversity of support for the credit union and to build acceptance of the need for unified action.

Efforts were also undertaken by local leadership to gain access to outside resources and to speak on behalf of the community. When application for the credit union stalled in Washington, DC, a bus trip to the nation's capital was arranged, and key supporters lobbied heavily on behalf of the fledgling organization. The final incorporation of the credit union provided a success in the community through diverse individuals and groups working together to achieve a common goal.

The credit union did not last long on its own. It merged with the Triborough Federal Credit Union on May 1, 1987, and it would be difficult to assess the long-term benefits of the organizing activity for Homestead itself. A comprehensive effort such as that in Aliquippa did not seem indicated, since Homestead already had human service organizations and its own community development organization.

THE MON VALLEY DEVELOPMENT TEAM

It is important to note that organizing activity and community-rebuilding efforts continued after the merger of the credit unions. Mike Eichler went on to found the Mon Valley Development Team, a group of community development specialists and community organizers who went out into the community to create new community development corporations (CDCs) and to provide technical assistance to these CDCs as they took on economic development projects. Four CDCs already existed in the Valley. The development team brought more than ten more into being, eventually working to build and provide technical assistance to 17 CDCs throughout the Mon Valley. Community-organizing activity was viewed as a central component in the work of the team. Patricia McElligott, a long-time community organizer, was hired to direct the organizers' efforts. Jo DeBolt, a specialist in small business development, was a principal in the economic development wing of the team. The Development Team staff, providing technical assistance to Homestead's community development corporation, helped to launch the first major project: a building rehabilitation project in Homestead's central business district.

Local leaders continue to be involved with community development project efforts. Mike Eichler went on to work for the Local

Initiatives Support Corporation (LISC), taking the Mon Valley Development Team concept to other cities across the country. More recently Mike became president of the Consensus Organizing Institute (COI), which continues to take the Mon Valley Development Team model and test it in other localities. COI is also interested in organizing activities beyond the scope of CDCs, and hopes to work more broadly with other types of organizing efforts. Homestead's community development corporation, and the other CDCs developed by the Development Team, continue to push for changes in their own communities and also work together in the Mon Valley Initiative, the successor to the Mon Valley Development Team. Jo DeBolt serves as the director of the Mon Valley Initiative. Patricia McElligott now works as a program officer in community and economic development for the Heinz Endowments, which from the beginning have provided major funding to the Mon Valley Initiative and the AAUD.

The Mon Valley Initiative is now a large program with substantial funding and fund-raising abilities. In the interview with Jim Cunningham in the last chapter of this book, the Mon Valley Initiative and its status and influence in the Valley are assessed. Clearly it is a force to be reckoned with.

To return to the credit union project, it confirmed the value of direct assistance to distressed communities for knowledge building. As in Aliquippa, positive community forces were present to be tapped. There were sufficient remnants of the social fabric in both communities even in the wake of serious economic downturn. The River Communities Project saw the credit union as another confirmation of the importance of latent community strengths and local leadership. Further, the community organizers working to establish the credit union were a source of in-depth information on social and economic distress in Homestead.

The selected examples of supported projects produced different prototypes for community organization, depending on the goals selected as appropriate. In both Homestead and Aliquippa, there were lasting effects that reached beyond the specific communities. The credit union organizing provided at least one organizer with the knowledge of a community and its leadership that was needed to launch another effort–the Mon Valley Development Team. The Aliquippa Alliance, intensely and densely focused on the mill town as it was, also contributed to demonstration efforts carried out in other mill towns. Among these were the the youth demonstration projects featured in the next chapter.

Chapter 14

The Youth Enterprise Demonstration Projects

The dramatic loss of young, skilled people and the lack of opportunities for the young people left behind, trends emerging repeatedly in the studies in southwestern Pennsylvania, called into question the region's future. Communities that were replacing local markets with boarded storefronts faced a grim prospect. It is not surprising that local organizations, trying to deal with the complex difficulties facing their residents, would begin looking at the viability of the future workforce. It seemed a good time to consider new programs and initiatives that might address both the immediate loss of young people and the need for new enterprises.

Denys Candy, a native Irishman with a masters degree in community organization from the School of Social Work, was a central figure in initiating some youth enterprise demonstration projects in Pittsburgh. In a newspaper interview, he recalled a trip home to Ireland in 1985: "I was introduced to young people starting their own businesses. I thought the concept could work here . . . when I got back, I called Jim Cunningham and said 'Jim, we've got to do this.'" (Rischell, 1989). Professor Cunningham liked the idea. So did organizers and developers working with other community groups already considering other kinds of youth programs.

Proposals were drafted to launch an interrelated youth enterprise demonstration project in three disparate, distressed communities in the region: Aliquippa, East Liberty, and Monessen. Researchers at the School of Social Work drafted a plan to evaluate the implementation of the work in order to facilitate funding; the plan was designed to record what happened, to note what appeared to work or not to work, and to discover what might be transferable to other distressed communities. Professor James Cunningham served as principal investigator for the evaluation of these projects, and Pamela Twiss was the evaluation project coordinator. In September 1988, the Appalachian Regional Commission funded the three projects. A press conference held in November 1988 announced the award of the funding, and an article in the *Pittsburgh Press* titled "Aid aims to halt exodus of youths" described the mission of the new program (Perlmutter, 1988). Three community groups and the University of Pittsburgh would divide $127,000 from the Appalachian Regional Commission to develop training programs for local youth.

In each of the communities initiating youth enterprise projects, a local group or organization sponsored and developed a program to recruit and train at least 15 young people to launch youth-owned or youth-operated enterprises or cooperatives during a two-year period (1988-1990). By and large, the common denominators to the projects start and stop there.

ALIQUIPPA

Aliquippa's economically and socially disadvantaged young people had been targeted for special assistance by a number of programs developed by the Aliquippa Alliance for Unity and Development, reported on in the previous chapter. A large summer youth employment project had been started. Innovative programming linked the city's disadvantaged youth to the community's elderly–a collaboration that promoted the well-being of older residents and addressed problems between the two populations. The young people also carried out marketing research and uncovered needs for businesses and services locally. A special enterprise development project geared to disadvantaged youth was a logical next step for the Alliance, a program that could readily be adapted to existing unique efforts.

The bulk of the training in Aliquippa was carried out in the local high school during study halls. Young people who had taken part in the previous summer's youth employment project became recruits for the in-school project. Other high-school-age youths were attracted to this school project through advice from the high school guidance counselors, advertisements, word-of-mouth, and visits by trainers to hangouts in the community. Sixty-five youths started the in-school project; 21 completed the training. The other 44 did not complete the training because they had difficulties with their schedules, were dropped from training for attendance or behavior problems, or could not maintain their grade point averages.

A project coordinator, D E'Andre Abercrombie, and a project counselor, Jennifer Henderson Milliner, conducted all of the in-school sessions, working with the youth in small groups of three or four at a time. Working in small groups turned out to be essential. The trainees had more serious literacy and numeracy problems than had been anticipated. Having the recruits put together individual business plans was soon recognized as an unrealizable goal. The trainers did not have complete control of the classroom environment, either. School administrators could cut study halls unexpectedly for early release or students could be called out of study halls for various reasons. The trainers attempted to compensate for these losses by offering makeup sessions and then by offering additional enterprise training throughout the following summer's youth employment program.

At the close of the project, much had been learned by the young people and their trainers. The young people enjoyed having the training during the study hall hours, but wished they could have met more often and that there were more participants. They recommended that any youths involved in future enterprise training also take part in the summer youth employment project, and that the two projects be systematically linked so that both experiences were provided. The Alliance saw an opportunity to reshape the enterprise training experience to provide more of what the youth needed, both to remedy their educational deficits and to foster their interests in entering the workforce. The Alliance began setting up its own sheltered enterprises where interested youth could seek work experiences while continuing their training. The ultimate goal: young people becoming coowners of the enterprises and cooperatives in which they worked.

EAST LIBERTY

An urban inner-city neighborhood that suffered disinvestment and blight, East Liberty has undergone significant social and economic change in the past 40 years. A huge urban renewal project, undertaken in the 1960s, isolated the neighborhood's business district and left its merchants with little access to shoppers. In the early 1980s, the city finally returned the area to its prerenewal state and reopened the business district to local automobile travel. An organization representing much of the community's business and real estate interests, as well as its civic and religious bodies–East Liberty Development, Inc. (ELDI)–spearheaded the drive to undo the failed infrastructure of the 1960s and renew the business district. ELDI also sought to aid new business starts and attract enterprises to the area, focusing its attention particularly upon minority- and women-owned enterprises.

In the 1980s, ELDI also began considering the future workforce in the community and launched several projects targeting local youth. The JobLink program, which was designed to provide employment in local businesses and services, was developed. Collaborative efforts with churches and human service organizations launched special in-school programs to prepare youth for a changing workplace and keep them in school. An enterprise project aimed at disadvantaged young people was the next step for ELDI, and a proposal for a youth enterprise project was developed and work begun with local organizations to launch the project's special training.

Two training sessions were developed, one each for high-school-age youth and for low-income adults. Ten students and 15 adults were recruited. By the end of the project, there were only four students still working together, and fewer than ten adults attended sessions regularly. Some accommodations were made to retain trainees. Two from the original high school group participated in the adult training due to scheduling problems, and one woman carried out her course work in her home due to transportation and child care problems.

The training for both high school and adult groups was the same. One trainer, Louise Craighead, was present for all sessions, a classroom format was used, and participants were expected to submit written materials regularly and also to develop a business plan for an enterprise that might be started locally. For those in the high school group, however, the plan was to be a joint venture, a cooperative or some other group enterprise that would provide hands-on application of course materials. Some members of the adult group were to have access to employment in a community recycling cooperative launched by ELDI, providing a number of them with similar hands-on experience and an opportunity later for cooperative ownership. Some of the men originally interested in working with the recycling co-op, however, dropped out. Another man chose to pursue recycling as a sole proprietorship after receiving training in how to manage a recycling venture. At the close of East Liberty's project, the high school group had run an ice cream vendorship as a cooperative, operating throughout the summer months. Several adults were working to finalize their business plans and launch new enterprises in the community but had not yet reached actual start-up.

As in Aliquippa, much was learned from the experience by both the participants and the program managers. The trainers would choose a simpler curriculum in the future and offer greater leadership and direction to high-school-age youth. The sponsoring organization would like to see future programs offered within and by the local school district so that it might concentrate its own efforts on launching new enterprises designed by already trained youth and young adults. Finally, the young adults who participated would like the benefits of hands-on training and greater application of the principles they learned prior to attempting to begin their own businesses.

MONESSEN

Another mill town, located in the mid-Mon Valley portion of the region, Monessen entered the late 1980s facing problems shared by Aliquippa: an aging and drastically reduced population, the loss of youth, and a dwindling tax base and failing commercial district. While Monessen did not have a large community-based recovery organization like the Alliance or a firmly rooted community development corporation like ELDI to sponsor projects such as a demonstration youth enterprise project, it did have interested local residents and an organizational leadership interested in new ideas and programs. A steering committee, led by the local school superintendent, Tom Wilkinson, was developed after a longtime resident and businessman, Martin Dudas, expressed a willingness to fund a youth enterprise project locally. Dr. Dudas' seed funding attracted additional monies from other foundations and corporations, and a pilot program was begun. Its target was relatively skilled young people with ideas for enterprises who might be prevented from joining the exodus of youth fleeing the valley in search of jobs and opportunities elsewhere.

Through this pilot program, seven young people were trained in enterprise development. Two immediately launched new enterprises and were set up, with great fanfare, on the main street of the business district in a building renamed the Enterprise Center. The two fledgling businesses received a lot of publicity in the days and weeks following the openings. There was great hope that other trainees pursuing their own ventures would soon follow suit. The project steering committee submitted a proposal to the Appalachian Regional Commission for a continuing youth enterprise project modeled after the initial demonstration program. Simultaneously, the local school district began seeking funding to offer an in-school training program to high-school-age youth as part of its changing curriculum. Funds were obtained for both programs.

Though formally and informally linked to one another, the in-school and out-of-school programs that were developed in Monessen were separately funded and administered, and each emerged with quite different outcomes. The out-of-school program was launched by and supervised by the steering committee that had supervised the first demonstration program in the community. The in-school program, offered as a course for credit in the local high school, was administered by the school district.

The out-of-school program was designed for young people who had an idea for an enterprise that they wanted to start locally, who already had some work experience, and who had shown acceptable academic performance. The program attracted precisely the young people it sought but not in large numbers. Originally 15 expressed an interest in the program. Of these, nine completed the application process and actually entered training. All nine had had some work experience, were at least high school graduates, and had ideas for businesses or services that they felt were needed in their community. Of the nine, seven completed the training and two were operating an enterprise when the program ended.

The training for the out-of-school program was conducted in the evening at the Enterprise Center, the site of the two small businesses launched by the previous pilot program. Sessions were conducted by consultants and local experts with experience in whatever they were teaching: counselors teaching stress management and how to assess personal strengths and weaknesses; accountants teaching record keeping; development specialists teaching actual start-up activities. The focus was on applied learning. Each recruit had to develop a market research strategy, carry out relevant research, develop a business plan, and when appropriate develop prototypes for products to be manufactured. In 1989, Tom and Amy Rapp, graduates of the program, were running O'Toole's Business Supply and Service Store, a once stable but recently declining old business in the heart of downtown Monessen. They took over the business from Amy's father. While Tom made service calls, Amy managed the shop. At the closing session of their training in the summer of 1989, the two talked about their plans for the future: Get the shop out of the red, diversify their services by joining a network of machine service shops, and add business support services to the shop, such as fax, word processing, and photocopying.

One graduate of the pilot program, Chris Cannizzaro, also started operating his own business, a luncheon service, two years after his training ended. This business, and that of the Rapps, represent the successes. As of 1989, the two businesses that had emerged from the pilot program (businesses that had given support to the larger out-of-school program) joined the other business failures in the area and folded in the first year of the larger program's operation. The Enterprise Center closed when funding for the youth enterprise project ended. Discouragement and disappointment followed for some on the pilot project's steering committee. With the Enterprise Center closed and the steering committee dissolved at the end of the second year of training, there would be no support for any trainees in need of technical support in the future.

The in-school project had little in common with the out-of-school program. It recruited all kinds of students: those excelling in school, those doing poorly, those who were considered "problems" in their classes, those with previous interests in business, and those in non-traditional classroom training. What did these young people expect to get from the class? What did they think an entrepreneur was? Alta Rusman, in her report on the in-school program, notes that the school's principal found the students unrealistic at first: "[T]hey painted a glowing picture of the life of an entrepreneur. The advantages they cited were: hiring others to work and doing very little yourself, driving around in a Cadillac, and retiring–young and rich–to Florida" (Rusman, 1990, p. 12).

The students soon realized that they had been unrealistic. The course was offered for a grade, attendance was required, and there were homework, out-of-school activities, and the hands-on experience of designing and launching an in-school business for at least a day. All sessions were taught by the same woman, an experienced business teacher, Vicki Furnier. The class started out with 30 students from a much larger pool of interested young people in the high school. At the close of training, two in-school businesses were operated at a profit for one day. The trainees involved felt that the learning really began that day. Everything went wrong that could go wrong. Some decided that being in business for themselves was not for them. Others decided that they wanted to pursue the possibility again some time in the future.

The two interrelated but distinct programs brought those involved in running the projects a great deal of knowledge, and some strong sentiments as to what they would do if they had to do it all over again. Tom Wilkinson, intimately involved with both projects in Monessen, remained very enthusiastic about youth enterprise and, when last contacted in the early 1990s, believed that both projects continued to have some life in the community. If he had it to do all over again, however, he would change a few things, particularly for an out-of-school program. Wilkinson sees a need to think more about the sponsoring committee or supporting organization for such a program. He would advise making sure that volunteers have substantial time to commit and that enough of them are really connected to the community undertaking the program. Though he would not change the way the in-school program was done, it was not a simple program to get started or keep going. Initially, the program was not supported by the school board. Wilkinson wishes he could change the perception of such programs. The tax base continues to shrink in Monessen, making it difficult to fund new or special programs such as those of the youth enterprise project, which are seen as frills. The fight to get the school board to continue the in-school program made it clear that the demonstrated merit of a program is not all that has to be considered when resources are diminishing.

In hindsight, Denys Candy, the director of the out-of-school program, sees too great a burden being placed on the young people to succeed in opening their own businesses. Candy would design a five-year strategy to focus on enhancing the overall education of the community's youth rather than just on entrepreneurship. He would seek support for such a long-term project in a broad-based community organization with a history in the community.

Gerald Dill of the local United Way was a committed supporter of the project and the programs, and he was on the steering committee in Monessen. He saw problems rooted in the provincialism and fragmentation of the community. Although people acknowledged that there was nothing for young people to do in the community, problems associated with that were not identified nor were possible solutions tackled. Dill asserted that "a number of groups keep stabbing at the problem," referring to such groups as the United Way, the Chamber of Commerce, and the Rotary, but said that there is no organized effort. It takes only a little disappointment or setback, he added, for people to decide that "it's just not going to happen here."

What were the common denominators and findings among these three communities and the multiple projects launched in each? All three communities struggled to overcome the helplessness that they experienced as they attempted to work in novel ways in the vacuum left by the demise of dominant institutions: big industry in the mill towns and government in the inner city. They all faced the dual problems of fragmentation and scarce resources in traditionally quite provincial communities with little experience in unified action. The community workers engaged in these three projects saw youth enterprise as a means of combatting the effects of the absence of dominant institutions and getting young people to think about–and rethink–their futures and those of their hometowns.

In evaluating the in-school program in Monessen, Alta Rusman, a writer unaffiliated with the design or implementation of any of the programs, concluded that the enterprise project was very important to youth participants in offering an opportunity for them to think creatively about their futures. In her words:

Each student had a unique experience. But they all came away knowing the ingredients that go into making a business succeed. Most important, they all gained a sense of themselves in the workplace. And with that new sense of self came a precious gift: the gift of knowledge that they can make choices, choices that will shape their careers and their lives. (Rusman, 1990, p. 5)

There is no doubt that this happened to many participants. But was that enough? The projects student participants devised showed promise but lacked sufficient support and resources. Could they or others have accomplished what was asked of them in such distressed communities? All of those involved, by the close of all three projects, agreed that any community choosing to undertake such programs needs to root them in a much broader effort to first bring the community together to fight for survival, job creation, and unity. With a strong local organization in place, committed to restoring the community and backed by local residents, a carefully designed project has a chance. Under those conditions, the other elements that were discovered to be critical to success, if implemented, may bring significant benefits.

The overall consensus seemed to be that the approach to youth was essential for the future, but required a broader, stronger, longer commitment. Youth enterprise, if it were attempted again, would begin with the support and supervision of a comprehensive, community-wide organization working in cooperation with the local school district. Young people, high school students as well as young adults, would have access to multiple facets of a project operated both within the local high school and outside of school. High-school-age youth would receive stipends and/or classroom credit for their training. Training would involve the use of expert teachers and offer ample opportunity for hands-on experience, preferably real work experience for pay in an enterprise that could either be spun off into employment elsewhere or developed as a cooperative after sufficient training and time on the job. Finally, projects would be designed to continue for a minimum of five years and the local sponsoring organization would be responsible for providing access to technical assistance that might be needed in the years after training, years when ideas long on the drawing board might finally materialize. Those working on the projects would also focus less upon enterprise development and more upon experiences that integrate learning and application in such a way that the workforce of the future is enhanced. Whether graduates moved into enterprises or not, they would be stronger, better-prepared workers, with a greater sense of who and what they can become.

Chapter 15

The River Communities Project
Seminar Series

In the fall of 1988 and the first months of 1989, the School of Social Work, led by the project executive committee, presented a series of six seminars in the Provost's Suite on the second floor of one of the major buildings of the University of Pittsburgh, the Forbes Quadrangle. Known as the Seminar Series, these seminars constituted the major vehicle for marking the close of project activities. After five years, the time had come to review research and demonstration results and to set the stage for a discussion of outcomes and policy perspectives with as large and varied a group of local parties as could be mustered. Since the preceding chapters covered all of the research projects plus selected examples of demonstration projects, the story of the Seminar Series need not recapitulate this earlier material. Instead, this chapter focuses primarily on a major mission of the project, agreed upon from the start: dissemination of the results. The Seminar Series was only one of the ways in which information and ideas were exchanged, but the series took place at a time when the material was still fresh and yet detailed results were available. Considerable time and thought was devoted to making the series a success. Success meant sharing as much as possible with as many as possible in a time frame and atmosphere conducive to broad participation. What was decided, how the series was implemented, and the results of the effort are the topics considered in this chapter.

The planners of the series were fortunate in having had a "practice" conference in the spring of 1987 that provided some guidance. An earlier conference, organized just as the River Communities Project was formally launched, became in hindsight a sort of rehearsal for the later seminars. On April 29, 1987, the members of the Strategies and Tactics course in conjunction with the School of Social Work as a whole presented *Can Pittsburgh Make It?*, a conference featuring Dr. Harvey Brenner of Johns Hopkins University as the keynote speaker. The leaders of the conference planning had been inspired by Brenner's work relating social and economic change to physical and mental health rates (Brenner, 1979; Brenner, 1980; Brenner, 1987). The presentation by Brenner was a fitting "opening gun" for the project, drawing attention as it did to the severe consequences of unemployment on a large scale.

Dr. Leon Haley, the President and Chief Executive Officer of the Urban League, was the main Pittsburgh speaker, highlighting the impact of unemployment on black residents of the area. Other local notables, in addition to the Dean, several faculty members, and numerous students from the school, were featured in or participated in discussion groups and workshops during the full day of the conference. The spotlight throughout was on unemployment, its consequences, and the challenges economic disaster offered in various human life spheres. A broad spectrum of local people from various agencies and towns and neighborhoods directly affected by the unemployment crisis attended the conference. The response was enthusiastic and many participants voiced an eagerness to receive more information about the local scene. Lessons were learned in that event that helped to make the later Seminar Series well-publicized, well-attended meetings.

Probably the most important thing that was learned was that packing too much material into a small space was a poor strategy. While the conference was certainly well received, many questions were only partially answered or not responded to at all because of time constraints when the conference ended. For the Seminar Series, it would be preferable to restrict each seminar to a focus on one research or demonstration project, even if this meant that not all projects could be included. Given the limits on faculty and student time during the fall and early spring months, and the always limited monetary resources of the River Communities Project, six seminars were considered the limit of feasibility. Six seminars, restricted to one project at a time, did not allow for all the projects to be presented. Six seminars, however, did allow time to present the projects selected in the desired detail with ample time for questions to be raised and for discussion to occur. It was decided that six seminars, each scheduled for two and one-half hours, would constitute the Seminar Series, and that there would be a mix of the formal action research projects from the second phase and demonstration projects. The choice of exactly which depended in some part on the availability of the major actors and their readiness to present during that time phase.

Among other things learned from *Can Pittsburgh Make It?* was the value of carefully planned early publicity with attractive packaging to ensure that people marked their calendars. Seminar brochures were designed in a slim folding four-page format on light blue paper with dark blue printing. Photographs taken in the mill towns were transposed to adorn the centerfold, using the same colors. The brochures were compact but they offered full information on the planned series in a limited space. The brochures announced the series title as *The Impact of Mass Unemployment on Communities, Families, and Individuals*: *Studies of Social and Economic Dislocation in the River Communities of Southwestern Pennsylvania During the 1980s*. The brochures were mailed well in advance of the first seminar in September 1988 to over 500 individuals and organizations, drawing in large part on the lists developed for the Brenner conference, and augmented by the suggestions for additional names provided by executive committee members and other members of the School of Social Work.

The brochures described the Seminar Series in these words:

> The findings to be presented in this seminar series grow out of five years of collaborative effort among university faculty, students, and staff and concerned local leadership in several battered industrial communities. The objectives of the effort include gathering and disseminating accurate information and informed opinion about the impact of severe social and economic change on people, institutions, and small communities, and from this search to help develop demonstration programs to advance recovery.

The dates of the seminars and the titles of the contents were also listed in the brochure. Under the dates, titles, and presenter names, credit was given to those who funded each particular project. The schedule read:

September 20, 1988   *The Impact of Social/Economic Change on Households: A Profile of Six River Communities*
Dr. Hide Yamatani, Dr. Lambert Maguire, Mr. Robin Rogers
This research was sponsored by a grant from the Pittsburgh Foundation.

October 18, 1988   *Creating an Entrepreneurial Culture for Youth in Industrial Towns in Southwestern Pennsylvania: The Youth Enterprise Demonstration*
Dr. James Cunningham, Professor Kiernan Stenson, Mr. Denys Candy, Mr. David Feehan
Funding for the Youth Enterprise projects has been provided by the Buhl Foundation, Martin M. Dudas Foundation, H. J. Heinz Foundation, Mon Valley Economic Revitalization Program, National Center for Neighborhood Enterprise, and the People's Natural Gas Company.

November 15, 1988   *When Unemployment Strikes Families: The Impact on Women*
Dr. Martha Baum, Dr. Barbara Shore, Ms. Kathy Fleissner
This research was supported by a grant from the Pittsburgh Foundation.

December 15, 1988   *The Unemployment Dilemma for the Elderly, Their Families, and Their Communities*
Dr. Mary Page, Dr. Myrna Silverman, Ms. Teresa Parton-Lopez, Ms. Betty Simonds, Ms. Audrey Spencer
This research was supported by a grant from the Pittsburgh Foundation.

January 17, 1989   *The Aliquippa Model for Community Recovery*
Ms. Cathy Cairns, Mr. Bill Farra, Dr. James Cunningham
Major funding for the Aliquippa community recovery effort has been provided by the Vira Heinz Endowment, Mellon Bank Foundation, Beaver Community Services Block Grant, Duquesne Light Company, Howard Heinz Endowment, Beaver County Human Services Development Fund, Beaver County Community Development Block Grant, Pennsylvania Legislature, Beaver-Butler Presbytery, the Catholic Diocese of Pittsburgh, and community donations.

February 21, 1989   *Fathers, Employment, and Child Care*
Dr. Phyllis D. Coontz, Dr. Judith A. Martin, Dr. Edward W. Sites
This research was supported by a grant from the Staunton Farm Foundation.

A detachable card that certified that "All seminars in the series are free and open to the public" was included in the brochure. Interested people were asked to check in the spaces provided on the card which seminars they planned to attend and return the card. The card was addressed to the school and was postpaid. All interested persons were welcome. The card simply served to give Seminar Series organizers some estimate of how many people planned to come to each seminar. Attendance at later seminars, that is, the ones occurring after September and October, was reinforced by special mailings to those on the initial list who might be especially interested in the topics of the later seminars.

The mailing list of about 500 to which the original seminar brochures were sent prominently featured:

- Social service providers
- Government officials (local municipal, county, state, federal)
- Advocates and advocacy organizations and hybrid organizations providing social services and also doing advocacy work

- Churches and church leaders from the region and affiliated social service organizations
- Community development individuals and organizations
- Academics from other schools/departments of the University of Pittsburgh and other colleges and universities in the area
- Participants in the projects as consultants, informants, and respondents

Space for the meetings was ample but not unlimited. The very large auditorium in the Forbes Quadrangle suite was arranged in rows of chairs stretching from side to side with tables, microphones, and slide equipment at the front. Entry to the auditorium was through a large anteroom of the suite, where entrants were given name tags, asked to sign a list with their names and organizational affiliations, and invited to sample refreshments. No one was refused entrance, although there was "standing room only" at several seminars. The atmosphere was kept informal, and it was possible only to keep a rough count of who came to what. The auditorium had a capacity of over 200 seats, and it was always filled and sometimes overflowing. While the presenters grouped up front for brief reports at the outset of each seminar, voices from the floor were soon encouraged, and participation was widely distributed among the members of the audience. Although 200 seats were sometimes not quite enough to seat everyone, the auditorium used did seem a good size to allow everyone to "get into the act."

The Dean of the school presided over the seminars whenever possible, and faculty and students not directly involved in presentations attended as well. Since term was in session, however, faculty and students had busy schedules and their participation was necessarily selective. Given the "full house" that prevailed at most seminars, the limited participation of faculty and students was to some extent an advantage, making room for participants outside the school. It almost goes without saying that it is very important to an enterprise like the seminars to have members of the press participate and publicize the proceedings. The members of the press were always personally invited to come to each seminar. Reporters from the two most prominent local newspapers, the *Pittsburgh Post-Gazette* and the *Pittsburgh Press* (now defunct), came regularly, and they wrote feature articles about the seminars that reached a wide local readership.

SUMMARY

All the evidence, then, suggested that the Seminar Series was successful in attracting, in large numbers, the people who could benefit most from the information disseminated. Members of the press spread the content of the individual seminars across the area in an indirect wave of positive publicity. The series was successful in another way too. Participants in the River Communities Project from the School of Social Work were exposed to an array of ideas from community members about the project and its impact on their communities. New insights into developments in the mill towns and the role of the school as perceived by the residents were freely voiced. The seminar participants also had many promising cooperative ventures of their own to report, as well as failed efforts. Much of the rich load of food for thought has been incorporated in the retrospective reflections of Part Six.

PART SIX:
THE RIVER COMMUNITIES PROJECT
IN RETROSPECT

The first chapter in Part Six takes a direct, critical look at the inner workings of the River Communities Project, assessing its organization, ongoing management, and general strengths and weaknesses. A second focus in Chapter 16 is on school-community relations, and some of the gains and risks in joint efforts are analyzed from both perspectives. Insights gathered in the process of carrying out the project may help other schools and departments (and communities!) to decide whether to become involved in stepped-up collaborative efforts and, if so, what tactics to use under particular conditions. A dose of self-criticism is necessarily introduced in making points that inform both academic and community leaders and assisting them to avoid pitfalls and make wiser choices. Simple observations and examples are used to illustrate some lessons learned.

Chapter 17 is intended to use reflective, retrospective thinking to do something else: provide policy themes at the micro level that emerged from the action research and show how some were put into operation and even became a part of community life. At the same time the limits to micro level interventions when confronted with an economic desert became clear. Neither a resourceful community nor an energetic school nor both working perfectly together can overcome the consequences of neglect by state and federal agencies at strategic times. It is a hard lesson to learn for those who worked so tirelessly to revive the stricken communities, but in this chapter we revisit Aliquippa and the Alliance for Unity and Development as a prime example of grassroots limitations. In communities where economic catastrophe occurs, community and social work efforts must place a first priority on enlisting macro interventions. There will still be an enormous need for social workers in concerted efforts with community leaders and residents to form coalitions at the community level to establish priorities, ensure that resources are used wisely, and help recovery along.

Chapter 16

Lessons Learned:
A Critical Analysis

The River Communities Project had multiple aims and purposes. The beginnings can be traced to the work of one professor and a class of social work students. The center of the project was to use a principal academic mission, research, and put it at the service of struggling communities in an economically deeply troubled region. Beyond this basic aim, a second goal was to provide direct assistance to community self-help groups. Overall, though, the project was many things to many people. For some students, it was an avenue through which to gain research experience, research credits, and opportunities to publish with faculty members. For faculty, it was a chance to pursue research interests, to bring new material into the classroom, and to publish. For both students and faculty, it was an opportunity to learn more about getting involved with communities in pain, to practice social work skills in a setting beyond the classroom and the field placement. For both groups, too, there was the goal of translating research findings into community action.

For some community groups, the project was a friendly partner with which to develop projects and seek funding for demonstration projects. For other groups and organizations, the River Communities Project was sometimes a source of needed or desired information, a facilitator, a resource broker. Alternatively, the project was viewed as a source of unwelcome information, an irritant, and a competitor. Such diverse views are not unexpected. Any project seeking to fulfill the aims of academe and community service simultaneously is as likely to win reproach as praise. The purpose in the beginning of this chapter is to think through the strengths and weaknesses and gains and losses of the project. Both the internal life of the university and the external life of the community are considered with a focus on where problems might be avoided for others pursuing action-oriented research and supporting demonstration projects in particular communities. The focus of the River Communities Project was on economic disaster, and unfortunately economic disasters are common in the United States today.

The River Communities Project had, from its beginnings, the strong support of the Dean of the School of Social Work. Dean Epperson served as the chair of the executive committee of the project, and involved himself in the day-to-day life of the overall project. He is a well-known figure in the greater Pittsburgh community, heavily involved in community service organizations and performing other functions benefiting community members. The significance of the active participation of the Dean was not lost on faculty, involved community organizations, and funding sources. His backing made it far easier to launch and maintain the project and to secure financial and other resources.

The project similarly benefited from strong support and widespread participation among faculty in the school. As noted previously, approximately half of the faculty served as principal or coprincipal investigators in the research projects or as regular members of the executive committee or both. They also pursued funding opportunities, worked with community organizations, supervised students working in the field, analyzed data, wrote reports, and presented the findings from the projects undertaken in seminars and other contexts. It was also primarily faculty who recruited students to participate in project activities and enlisted colleagues from other schools and disciplines to contribute to the research activities. The time and effort faculty members spent on research and other project requirements was not reimbursed by funding received; it was donated. Faculty during this time continued to fulfill their normal teaching and administrative obligations. In short, faculty choosing to take on these research efforts showed commitment to community service by the sacrifices they made. The only tangible gains that could possibly be received in return were juried publications in the future, which were by no means guaranteed.

The committee-style administration of the River Communities Project, with the Dean as chairperson, brought together key administrative staff and some of the faculty working on research projects. The committee was a working committee with serious responsibilities. It determined policy for the project, reviewed grant proposals prior to submission to potential funders, reviewed project reports before they were published in final form, and guided the direction of the project. The committee form of administration worked very well and proved to be quite flexible, meeting more often when necessary, meeting less often during slow periods. Communication lines among committee members were open and fluid; minutes from the meetings kept members abreast of activities and were circulated to noncommittee member faculty at strategic points.

The structure also had its weak points. Although faculty were well represented, the executive committee structure did not emerge from broad discussion among faculty and administrative officers. Members were invited by the Dean. Half of the members were faculty, but they were not chosen because they were working on projects, although most did become involved in writing proposals and sometimes also in the projects that were selected. There were more faculty serving as principal investigators or coinvestigators who were not on the committee, although these faculty were invited to meetings related to the specific project on which they were working. As there were no regularly scheduled meetings of investigators, however, in hindsight communication among the people most centrally involved in action research projects suffered.

If the River Communities Project were to be started over, further consideration would be given to the selection of members for the executive committee. To get the project started and to provide continuity throughout the project, it was probably wise to begin with and maintain a carefully chosen group that was not unwieldy in size. The committee, however, could be expanded in size to include investigators and coinvestiators when several projects were in the design and implementation phase, and then contracted again as the projects in process got under way. Faculty do not want or need more meetings, especially when their loads are being increased through voluntary efforts. But enhanced communication and sharing among investigators and coinvestigators would definitely be an asset, in the final analysis, lessening the burden and improving the results. Minimally, regular meetings among investigators and staff working on individual projects in the early phases should be arranged. All those involved on any of the projects could help one another with common tasks: developing samples, assembling data collection instruments, planning data collection strategies, and hiring and training interviewers or other needed personnel for data collection.

It is obvious in the preceding chapter on study findings that common threads emerged in the research, in particular a focus on the impact of massive unemployment and a focus on social support networks. These crosscutting findings were not systematically planned but arose serendipitously from the mutuality of interests among social work faculty and familiarity with the objectives of the River Communities Project. Heightened systematic contact among the faculty involved would have led to a greater sharing of approaches and, most important, to more precision in comparability of findings. This mutually planned approach is not to produce standardization, but rather to ensure that similar data are collected around key themes so that similarities and differences among target figures and groups can be delineated and intervention strategies sharpened. It would also be a good idea for many of the same reasons for the faculty involved to regather when the data have been collected to help one another with decisions about data analysis.

AN ANALYSIS
OF SCHOOL-COMMUNITY RELATIONS

The School of Social Work at the University of Pittsburgh celebrated its jubilee in the 1980s. During those 50 years many forays by faculty and students into the field have been made. Many relationships, including long-standing ones with a number of organizations and community groups in the mill towns, have resulted. Graduates of the school manage and staff organizations in which current students have their placements and practicums. The strengths of relationships developed over the years are evident. The school is fed by the experiences of students in the field; new techniques and trends in practice are often shared through classroom presentations of students; and students often report on new socioeconomic developments in specific areas in the region. Faculty are invited to sit on boards in the communities; organizational leaders are invited to sit on the committees of the school.

School-community interactions are mutually beneficial. Between the School and the community, there are mutual interests and objectives. The historical linking of school and community does not come without problems. This becomes apparent particularly where regional change is dramatic and where attempts to develop new organizations and institutions are being undertaken. Enduring relationships may lead to broad familiarity with some organizations and institutions external to the school at the cost of acquiring very limited knowledge of other, especially newer, less conventional groups. As a result, newer organizations and institutions may view the established relations between the school and the community as a sort of old boy network. This perspective leads to questions as to why projects, especially projects that involve funding, go where they go. The issue is most critical when demonstration projects are developed. There is a perceived possibility that an initial infusion of money will establish a long-term project and lead to greater strength or capability in one or two organizations among a larger group with similar interests. Any other organization performing activities centrally or peripherally involved with the aim of the demonstration is likely to feel that it has been slighted or cut out of an important funding opportunity. The Youth Enterprise Demonstration Projects, for example, created protests as to "why there and not here." The issue was dealt with in various ways and with varying degrees of success. Groups already involved in training youth served in an advisory capacity to the demonstration projects in some communities; in other situations they were consulted with and sometimes asked to become partners in future efforts. Successful efforts led to the development of real partnerships and joint ventures. But sometimes groups involved in training youth were not pacified, and there was at least some community feeling that the groups were just being used or offered "paper participation."

Community organizations working with the school had to deal with competition in other ways. In a desperately poor community, even a very small infusion of funds for a demonstration effort represents opportunity. Following the initiation of youth programs in one community, a number of groups decided that they too would offer demonstration projects. The organization with the greatest experience was faced in this situation with determining whether to recognize these new endeavors and decide how they might work together, to work with some and ignore others, or to ignore them all and openly compete for funding. This is one example of how bad blood may be created among community groups and also how a potential project can be delayed or even prevented from implementation. Any school wishing to join forces with community organizations has to be fully aware that selective involvement carries with it both positive and negative judgments in the community. When money is very tight, yet time is of the essence, schools must make hard decisions as to where and in what ways and for what reasons they should become involved. Conflict between community groups is certainly to be avoided if at all possible when community members need to pull together.

Academic institutions must make other choices as well, choices that accompany action-oriented research. Working with community leaders and residents to improve the research focus, comprehensiveness, and targeting creates a desire to maintain good relations and also to congratulate those who are working hard to promote survival and renewal in the community. The goodwill subtly or not so subtly undermines the researchers' ability to critically analyze roles and functions of community groups working in partnership with a school. Certainly faculty and students working in the field side by side with community activists are likely to be predisposed to view positively what takes place there. Yet, ironically, it is only through such close work that faculty and students can sufficiently view the effort in its context to critique it appropriately, providing awareness of the seductive possibilities is maintained.

Some of the tendency to accentuate the positive can be effectively dealt with when teams of students and faculty work together, bringing multiple perspectives to the situation. If it is not possible to arrange a counterbalancing of views, then maintaining some distance and objectivity on the work of organizations is critical. Developing and sustaining such a position, although it is normative in academe, is difficult, especially if community groups in partnership with a school feel threatened by the objectivity. Program evaluation efforts by the School in the River Communities Project are a good example of the delicacy of the researchers' position. Faculty involved in program evaluations, even when their reports were 99.9 percent positive, could be accorded exceedingly hostile receptions in the community based on the minuscule negative content. The stance of the school was that criticism had to be provided wherever it was supported by evidence and verifiable. The stance in the community was that even the gentlest negative commentary by an evaluator could mean future cuts in or the loss of funding, even when the body of the report was almost entirely positive.

Schools are constantly facing the question "What are we to do?" The profession of social work, grounded in a commitment to social change and to activism, historically has necessarily taken risks, in research as well as in practice. Action-oriented research emerges from social work's professed goals. Action-oriented research also has roots in academic and institutional self-interest. James Cunningham, principal investigator of the River Communities Project, repeatedly stated: "As goes the region, so goes the school." Action-oriented research leads to greater risk-taking as it inspires community action with the attendant pitfalls. Given the advantages, however, a school of social work is likely to decide that the gains are worth the risks.

A major caution in undertaking the risks is the need to understand and constantly be mindful of the community and its desires for self-determination. There are some gains for community organizations that may occur through entering partnership with a school. For example, low- to no-cost technical assistance may be gained, or credibility with funders and government officials increased, when community concerns are backed up by evidence gathered by academics. At the same time the commitment required of community organization leaders in community-based research and demonstration is monumental. Although grants are always welcome, any evaluative components quite literally get in the way of the day-to-day operations of community programs. Community groups and organizations are caught in a terrible dilemma. They can get any useful sum of money in tight times only by seeking multiple grants from multiple funding streams. The grants are mostly short-term in nature. Each grant brings evaluation experts or funding officers or both to their offices, which distracts them from their work efforts. The pressure for accountability for funds can literally put community groups and organizations in a position where they cannot do their work because they are too busy proving they are accountable. Often grants provide no money for administrative overhead, and their accountability efforts are even more frustrating because the time goes unremunerated.

Community groups have to determine, on a case-by-case basis, whether involvement in a partnership with a school or university potentially brings gains or losses. This weighing and balancing by community organizers must be respected and also facilitated by discussing the advantages and disadvantages just outlined. The nature of the partnership, too, is an essential factor. Where relationships with a school are structured to enhance an enduring partnership, evolving over the course of many projects, gains will necessarily be more tangible. By contrast, where partnerships are developed on the basis of short-term projects for which there is no prospect of continued funding, the required input from the community may well outweigh the benefits of involvement. As a school must make choices, so must the community, and both should be commended for attempts to choose wisely and hopefully for the common good.

Chapter 17

Developing Micro Level Policy: Emergent Themes

Where do people turn when a whole way of life is lost, perhaps permanently? What can be done to help people caught in an economic disaster to maintain or regain emotional equilibrium? The studies that have been reviewed showed that, in the mill towns of southwestern Pennsylvania, people turned to their nearest and dearest in their informal networks. Family ties were uppermost, and those ties often crossed households and included two or more adult generations. The "modified extended" family showed great strength as adult children turned to parents for support, as in the research on the elderly, or there was a two-way street between adult parents and adult children, as in the women's study. Unemployed fathers depended on small family circles to help meet child care needs, for they distrusted nonfamily arrangements. In the six-community survey as well, it was most often to the family that afflicted members turned.

The family was there and the family helped in many ways. Without employment or with only inadequate employment for most of the households of the communities, however, there were limitations on what families could be expected to do. Some people did go to service agencies and to churches for support, and as far as the research documents, most people did get assistance if they asked for it, although not always as much as was wanted. Many respondents, however, made it clear that they preferred not to be dependent on formal agencies. Even when families revealed tension and stress among their members, there was reluctance to call in "outsiders" in these small communities where tightly knit ethnic and religious ties often prevailed. Especially mistrusted, it seemed, were community mental health centers. Their image as working with the mentally unbalanced sometimes ran up a red flag. Churches, on the other hand, were more acceptable as helpers, although the resources the churches exhibited were very limited, and respondents sometimes seemed almost apologetic about the "generosity" of the church.

Family links were the most binding, but also very vulnerable. It was helpful when the small links of families could be bound together at the community level. Researchers collected and discussed at the River Communities Project Seminars ideas respondents put forth, some of which were implemented at least at the multiple-household level. Women asked for more support or self-help groups that would transcend family members, and a mental health clinic in one town and a church in another made calls or visits to faculty in the school to seek advice about groups they were in the process of initiating. These groups met with some success, but only with women. Men were conspicuously absent even though special recruitment efforts were made. Other efforts to launch support groups may have been made with more success, but as far as the school was aware, persuading men from the mill towns to accept support from any formal source except job-training programs remained impossible throughout the project. Other possible options to produce mutual benefits in times of widespread trouble were advanced through the experiences of research respondents and discussed at the seminars and at community presentations. For example, on a small scale, household repair and replacement needs were being exchanged among neighbors in some areas. A cooperative movement organized at the community level for members to exchange skills and goods could have solved many household deficit problems. Another lack in some communities, especially voiced by women, was dependable, affordable child care. Without it, many women could not work, even though their families needed their financial contributions. A community cooperative effort could have killed two birds with one stone by offering employment for women in child care that would free other women for paid labor and other activities. Exchanges such as the ones mentioned above could have paid off handsomely. The research generally showed that there was a reservoir of people who were unemployed or underemployed who were longing to put their talents to use.

It needed special skills and energy to put community-wide exchanges together. The communities had those in the form of community leaders and organizers, social service agency professionals, and religious institutions. As reported in Part Five, in a number of mill towns projects at the community or subcommunity level were organized with support from the school, and accomplishments were realized in the short run at least. There was no shortage of caring people or imagination; there was a terrible shortage of financial resources.

The mill towns were faced with a downward spiral of resources that stifled efforts toward recovery. Once prosperous communities were losing on every front. Household income dropped precipitately and did not revive. Tax revenues for community maintenance became smaller and smaller. Mill towns could no longer afford even to maintain minimal infrastructures of paved streets and solid sidewalks. Far more worrisome to community members was the decline in services such as fire fighting and police protection. Crime was increasing, especially in the areas of drug trafficking, shoplifting, robbery, and arson, but the forces to combat these crimes were weakened. The population of the river communities was declining sharply, and those remaining in the area were frightened and often suspicious of one another. Racial tensions, already visible before the mills shut down, were exacerbated. Empty shops and abandoned buildings replaced once busy, well-lighted main streets. In many respects it is clear that the mill towns represented unpromising settings for community organization ventures or, for that matter, for new businesses.

The most successful of the community organization projects generated in the River Communities Project paradoxically illustrates the near impossibility of revitalizing a community that has been totally stripped of financial resources unless there is significant (and swift) financial help from state and federal governments. The Aliquippa Alliance for Unity and Development, a community organization effort first described briefly in Chapters 2 and 3, was initiated by Cathy Cairns, a graduate student in community organization, as a goal for her field placement. As noted earlier, she thoroughly documented her organizing efforts (Cairns, 1986; Cairns, 1991). Working with Cathy from the outset was Lorenzo Williams of the National Association for the Advancement of Colored People in

Aliquippa. Both received inspiration from research on Aliquippa by the School of Social Work, which included an organizing plan for community recovery. Research findings, however, did not receive a uniformly positive reception in Aliquippa. The mill town was noted for its controversial elements and many residents were averse to hearing any more "bad news" and angry that Aliquippa had been "singled out."

The organizing effort was agonizingly slow at first, but in July 1984 a breakthrough meeting of diverse groups in the community was arranged, which signalled the first positive step toward "unity." This sign of hope was welcome, for it took an initial year of holding public meetings before the Alliance became a going concern with an agreed-upon agenda. The first two agenda items were directly related to the disastrous and long-lasting unemployment. One item was identifying the types of services needed by local low-income families just so they could survive and finding where these services could be obtained. The other was the very predictable concern with grassroots initiatives that could lead to long-term creation of jobs and reinvestments (Cairns, 1991).

While the public hearings were going on, the Alliance began to address the community's historic racial tensions. A beginning was made by developing training programs for the mostly white police force and the minority communities and organizing multiracial festivals called Community Days. Things moved very slowly at first, but eventually representatives of many community groups, with all their diversities and animosities, began to work together. After the first year of effort, the Alliance had a name and had purchased and renovated a building on the town's major street with the help of 1,800 volunteer hours from unemployed steelworkers and retirees, male and female. By 1986 the Alliance had turned this building into a social service facility right in the heart of town and visible and accessible to all. Soon about 1,700 persons and families were being served every month. By the end of 1986 Mellon Bank, the major bank in the area, offered to donate one of its branch office buildings, which was in West Aliquippa, to Alliance activities. The Alliance accepted the donation and immediately began raising funds to convert the building into its planned small business incubator. The facility was renovated with the help of a grant from the Howard

Heinz Endowment, and it opened early in 1988 with seven initial tenants. Rentals were low and subsidized by grants from private foundations and community donations. Some of the new tenants brought in to start new businesses, however, were found to lack the necessary skills and experience, and so a predevelopment six-week training course was planned (Cairns, 1991).

Cairns (1991) noted that even as this setback was encountered, the Alliance experienced new organizational growth with the simultaneous development of two initiatives. Additional assistance from the Howard Heinz Endowment supported a demonstration of a large-scale youth enterprise project that was carried out simultaneously with a remedial education project tied to in-home services and nutritional programs for senior citizens. At that time the Aliquippa Alliance for Unity and Development also negotiated a successful merger with another local coalition, the Aliquippa Development Corporation, Inc. A number of spin-off programs were developed. For example, a graduate student from the School, Christa McClusky, coordinated the Coalition on Innovative Childhood Intervention to fund a mix of social service and education agencies to study child care, employment, training, and education needs through the year 2000. In a more immediate, practical vein, summer youth employment projects were organized in successive years so that remedial education was provided in a context in which young people were also paid to provide services to seniors in low-income households. Summer-employed youths were also assigned to do such things as central business district cleanups and neighborhood surveys of service needs (Cairns, 1991). The list of accomplishments for the Alliance goes on and on, and many organizations, including the Commonwealth of Pennsylvania, contributed to the effort. A number of students and faculty from the school became involved. Faculty from other universities and colleges all over the area also participated as researchers, consultants, and teachers.

The central person, however, in initiating and guiding the effort was Cathy Cairns, who began as the group's organizer, then became Board Chair, and eventually Executive Director. Cathy is the first to insist that, although she is proud of her leading role, the Alliance is ultimately the result of collective planning and constructive effort by many people and groups concerned about the future of Aliquippa.

Yet, in spite of all the strides that have been made, the amazing accomplishments against long odds, Aliquippa is still a struggling community. The population has stabilized. The survival programs (once thought temporary) are still needed to keep poverty from being even more savage; however, what is needed, and has been needed for a long time, is a retrained workforce, new employers willing to risk hiring newly trained workers at decent pay, a rehabilitated area where blight and crime are reduced, and much, much more (Cairns, 1991). The Alliance clearly will continue to strive for positive change, but the battle remains an uphill one. The Alliance for Unity and Development has been unusually successful in engaging and sustaining community cooperation and in obtaining human resources and financial support from multiple sources. Given the magnitude of the disaster, it has not been enough. Aliquippa began to heal itself some six or seven years after the massive unemployment in the wake of the loss of big steel. But without a revival of employment opportunities, Aliquippa remains locked in a high-stress struggle of attempted rebuilding and bare maintenance.

Chapter 18

The Limits of Micro Level Interventions: Looking to State and Federal Governments

The problem from the outset was massive unemployment. The people of the mill towns were accustomed to a self-reliant existence. There had been temporary layoffs in the past. That was part of working at the mills and the fluctuations of the economy. It was unthinkable, however, that the mills would close for good. The workers had not recognized their heavy dependence on just one major source of employment that when it went would take everything else with it. They were accustomed to large corporations and not to bootstrap operations. The residents of the mill towns thought that government agencies and other large corporations would be the sources of recovery. All that came, however, were job-training programs. As has been noted before, these programs were inadequate to the demand. Reluctant to accept public assistance and other kinds of aid, mill town unemployed and underemployed eagerly sought job training as a remedy for the situation. But the training slots were actually few, and even those who received training, usually the ones who needed it least, were not always helped.

Gradually community self-help efforts took place, for, in spite of cleavages among some groups, the mill towns had a sense of community identity and commitment, as evidenced in the data collected through the River Communities Project. Several communities organized, especially around the creation of jobs. One strong example was Duquesne, which set up the Duquesne Advisory Corporation, comprising local government, business, and church leaders. The local government had been very active in promoting economic development, particularly the reuse of the idle mill property. But this hard-hit community, like other mill towns, had become too unattractive to bring in large-scale outside employers. The mills themselves had been allowed to deteriorate to the point that they no longer appeared viable for operations.

Graduate students and faculty from the school were involved in several community job efforts such as the one described above, but the results were marginal. A few jobs were created here and there, and some former steelworkers set up their own businesses. Much more activity was needed for recovery, and great excitement was generated in April 1986 when Representative Charles Hayes, a Democrat from Illinois, visited the Croatian Center in Aliquippa to gather material for a congressional hearing on the Income and Jobs Action Act of 1985. As the *Pittsburgh Press* of April 18, 1986, reported: "The bill, H.R. 1398, sets full employment as a national goal, and proposes lower interest rates, increased public and private spending, plant closing guidelines, and adequate income for those able and willing to work even when opportunities are not available."

Members of the School of Social Work attended the hearing, and Jim Cunningham testified about the extent of unemployment in the river communities and the need for direct government involvement in jobs programs. Representative Hayes said that the bill had been called "a dream," and a dream it turned out to be. For in spite of local and national support and pressure from the Congress, such a bill had no chance under President Ronald Reagan. The mill towns continued to struggle on with almost exclusively local resources. The population continued to decline and also to age as young people lost hope of renewal and left.

A large-scale federal input in the form of job opportunities might have given the depressed economy the kind of jump start that would have given both the residents and the communities they lived in an impetus to recovery or at least partial recovery. It could have worked even when the Income and Jobs Action Act was before Congress in 1986 and 1987, although much of the infrastructure of the region was in drastic need of repair, and the communities were being drained of a large proportion of their labor force.

The greatest chance to salvage the mill towns and the people would have come through fast emergency legislation to provide relief. Missing for the river communities was a viable safety net. From the point in time that documentation of the destitution in the mill towns became available, both River Community Project members and community leaders expected the federal government to loosen requirements and speed assistance to the beleaguered communities. Nothing of the sort happened; applications for assistance were processed in a leisurely fashion, as if the economic situation were normal. In the study of the impact of household unemployment upon women, conducted in 1986 and 1987, specific mention was given to the need for an immediate response to areas suffering from economic distress:

> A rapid response with tangible assistance seems essential. Unemployment produced dramatic income losses for the study households. Jobs could not be replaced in an area from which the dominant industry on which most employment depended shut down or moved away. Families lost their incomes or had to watch them deteriorate. Access to medical care became precarious as employment was lost. The findings show that multiple losses applied to a variety of household types, as has been found in other studies (Brenner, 1976; Humphrey & Krannick, 1980). It is not surprising that near paralyzing anxiety was created in many families. If threats to survival of this magnitude are created by catastrophic stress, an immediate response package should be generated.
>
> The package would include minimally:
> A financial floor to all affected households;
> Rent and mortgage assistance to prevent housing losses;
> Quick, easy access to the medical assistance program (Medicaid) when medical coverage is lost.

These steps, which would protect families from the most immediate attacks on the quality of life, would necessarily stem from federal and state auspices under emergency legislation triggered by distress indicators. An indirect but very important and positive result would be to enhance cash flows into depressed areas which would benefit entire communities. Community resources would remain viable to maintain infrastructure and ensure community services. (Baum, Shore, and Fleissner, 1989, p. 31)

Given the unresponsiveness of the federal government and the already long duration of the economic collapse, attention was turned to the state, in this case the Commonwealth of Pennsylvania, as the next best source of relief for a stricken area. The emergency relief idea was formulated more explicitly and with more sophisticated guidelines and shared in the River Communities Project seminars and in meetings with key political leaders.

A very important contact was State Senator Michael Dawida, from the town of Homestead in the Mon Valley, who was highly concerned about the sufferings of the mill towns. Senator Dawida worked with the School of Social Work to develop a plan for legislation, which was unveiled at a conference titled "Building an Economic Disaster Shield for Pennsylvania Families." The conference was jointly sponsored by Senator Dawida and the School of Social Work at the University of Pittsburgh and held in the William Pitt Union (the student union) on the University campus. Cosponsors of the conference included some 15 diverse agencies and organizations:

- Steel Valley Providers Council
- Turtle Creek Providers Council
- Community College of Allegheny (South Campus)
- United Way of Allegheny County
- Office of Affirmative Action, University of Pittsburgh
- Community Human Services, Inc.
- Southwestern Pennsylvania Human Services, Inc.
- Greater Pittsburgh Community Food Bank, Inc.
- Community Organization Group of the School of Social Work, University of Pittsburgh
- Graduate School of Public and International Affairs, University of Pittsburgh
- Health and Welfare Planning Association
- Aliquippa Alliance for Unity and Development
- Student Executive Council of the School of Social Work, University of Pittsburgh
- Christian Associates of Southwestern Pennsylvania
- Lawrenceville Citizens Council

The conference was held on November 19, 1990. It brought together many interested parties for a day beginning at 8:30 a.m. and ending at 2:15 in the afternoon. Dean David Epperson gave the introductory speech and the body of the conference consisted of two workshops. According to the conference program distributed to the participants, the rationale, the proposed action, and the major purpose were as follows:

> Careful review of the (research) findings reveals many ways human devastation might be eased or even prevented during the next economic down turn, a down turn that may arrive soon given the fragile nature of the present economy. Such prevention needs to involve preparation and effort by both the public and private sectors. In a key position to build a comprehensive and coordinated prevention shield is the Commonwealth of Pennsylvania with its relevant programs in medicaid, unemployment compensation, employment services, training and education, housing, mortgage assistance, mental health services, children and youth services, public assistance, and a host of others.
> In addition, the Commonwealth has considerable experience in providing crisis coordination and tangible aid during natural disasters. This proposal would seek to ensure that widespread family economic disaster would receive the same attention as is now given to sudden and severe natural disasters, such as flood and tornado. The purpose of the conference is to launch a proposal for such a program, a proposal being developed under the leadership of State Senator Michael M. Dawida.

Two hour-long workshops followed the introductory remarks. The workshops each had a chairperson from the School of Social Work and panelists from the University of Pittsburgh and community organizations. The topic of the first workshop was "The Family: Impact of Massive Unemployment," and it was chaired by Professor Barbara K. Shore of the School of Social Work. One panelist was Professor Phyllis Coontz of the Graduate School of Public and International Affairs, who had been a coinvestigator on the unemployed fathers project. The other two panelists were Rob Rogers of the Allegheny County Commission on Workforce Excellence, and Marlene Schick of McKeesport Hospital. The three panelists were able to talk about the impact on families from different perspectives, leading to a well-rounded picture of family deprivation.

The second workshop had as its topic "The Community: Struggle for Survival and Recovery," a more comprehensive framework than that centered on the family. Professor Aaron Mann of the School of Social Work, who is heavily involved in work in the African-American community, chaired the second workshop. Again the panelists represented diverse perspectives. Two panelists were Elaine Carr and Diana Gilbert of the Aliquippa Alliance for Unity and Development. They were followed by Professors Lambert Maguire and Hide Yamatani, who carried out the large-scale survey for the River Communities Project. The final panelist was Tracy Soska, who at that time was with the Turtle Creek Providers Council. The response to the two workshops was overwhelmingly positive, and participants declared themselves ready to back action to alleviate the conditions families and communities undergo when economic disaster strikes.

At noon, Senator Dawida held a press conference. After that, conference participants joined together for a luncheon that featured a presentation by Senator Dawida on the proposed legislation, followed by supportive responses on behalf of the business and labor communities by prominent representatives of each. The audience was then invited to address questions to Senator Dawida. In a climate of widespread enthusiasm for the Senator's plan, the conference was then adjourned.

According to business editor James Rankin, writing in the *McKeesport Daily News,* Dawida's likening the economic plan to responses to natural disasters was apt. In his lead paragraph, Rankin made the following comments: "Figuratively speaking, the collapse of the domestic steel industry during the 1980s hit the Mon Valley like an earthquake. State Senator Michael Dawida of Homestead would like to see the state react as if such a disaster really happened."

In several subsequent paragraphs, Rankin went on to say: "During a press conference yesterday at the University of Pittsburgh, Dawida unveiled proposed legislation which he called a state 'economic disaster' program . . . Developed with the assistance of the School of Social Work at Pitt, the program would facilitate better coordination between existing state agencies for faster action in the event of severe economic recession or collapse" (Rankin, 1990).

The article in the *Daily News* then continued at some length with details on the economic triggers for the plan and the organization that would put the disaster relief into effect. It was noted that, although the plan was for future emergencies primarily, at least six mill towns would be eligible for immediate help.

Other newspapers reported on the legislative plan, and Senator Dawida began to enlist legislative colleagues to sponsor what appeared to be a popular method of intervening in state economic disasters. A draft of the proposed Family Economic Disaster Prevention Act of Pennsylvania, dubbed "An Act," was released on August 28, 1990, for distribution, revision, and eventual submission to the General Assembly of the Commonwealth of Pennsylvania for legislative action. The intent of the act, as stated in the draft's preface, was for "the Commonwealth of Pennsylvania to protect and promote the general well-being of the inhabitants of this Commonwealth by establishing a program for the coordination and emergency provision of assistance to families facing disaster due to severe economic recession."

The carefully crafted document buttressed the need for such a policy with convincing historical and current data, and spelled out the general purposes and specific functions to be implemented. The roles to be played by state officials and local committees were also indicated. The stage was set for early legislative consideration. But this plan also proved to be a dream, for it was never even placed on the agenda of the state legislature. Pennsylvania had been making up the shortfall from federal sources in order to maintain its public programs. At the same time the state had been managing to preserve a balanced budget. But the tragedy that had swept communities in Pennsylvania, the very type of tragedy at which the Family Economic Disaster Prevention Act was aimed, caught up with the state over time because of the persisting high demands on public programs. These demands were causing budgetary deficits by 1990, and the politicians and the citizenry were becoming alarmed. Legislation that might have been given a chance to be enacted a few years earlier became unthinkable in 1990.

Perhaps eventually such shields will be erected. In many parts of the United States, economic collapses have occurred and continue to occur that resemble what happened in the river communities of

Pittsburgh. Surely early intervention would be preferable in every way, including economically, to the wasteland that persists in the river valleys more than a decade after an economic catastrophe occurred.

Chapter 19

Epilogue:
A Few Last Observations
and an Interview with Jim Cunningham

While the state of Pennsylvania as a whole and the Pittsburgh region in particular have been improving somewhat economically in the past few years, the river community mill towns are still ravaged by high levels of joblessness and poverty well over a decade after the major mill shutdowns and permanent layoffs began. This final chapter will take a last look at the mill towns in relation to the most recent developments. The chapter focuses on three questions:

How are the mill towns doing today?
Is there a sequel to the River Communities Project?
What can be envisioned for the future of southwestern Pennsylvania?

THE MILL TOWNS TODAY

On May 14, 1993, Professors Hide Yamatani and James Cunningham published the third wave of *The Mon Valley Workforce Survey*. This report, completed toward the very end of the activities on the River Communities Project, was supported by the Mon Valley Progress Council, the Mon Valley Initiative, and the Pittsburgh Plate and Glass Foundation. The School of Social Work sponsored the survey, and the University Center for Social and Urban Research at the University of Pittsburgh conducted the sample selection, telephone interviews, and data entry components of the research.

In the introduction to the report, the authors state:

> Evidence of economic distress remains strong in the Mon Valley
> of Southwestern Pennsylvania where the ill effects of the reces-
> sion that began in 1990 have intensified weaknesses remaining
> from the collapse of the steel and coal industries in the 1980s.
> Current evidence, gathered in the University of Pittsburgh's 1993
> Mon Valley Workforce Survey of 1,201 residents reveals wide-
> spread employment difficulties, households without health bene-
> fits, a willingness among many to accept relatively low wages, a
> very small number of manufacturing jobs and many households
> considering a move out. Coupled with the U.S. Census recent
> announcement that this area lost 10 per cent of its population
> between 1980 and 1990, these factors mark the subregion as one
> in grave need of stepped-up planned economic development pro-
> grams. (Yamatani and Cunningham, 1993)

The report continues with more specific commentary on distress
and hardship in the Mon Valley. The authors note that the area has
been battered by social and economic negative changes over the past
14 years, and that the current report shows no improvement over the
earlier reports of 1988 and 1991. The residents in 1993 suffer from
one and one-half times the official unemployment rate of the four-
county market area of which the Mon Valley Communities are part.
A substantial number of residents have no health care and wages
generally are below the norm. Periods of unemployment for heads
of households often go beyond the limit of 26 weeks of state compensation. The worst off are African-American and single female
heads of households. The harsh employment picture and the population loss mark the area as one in desperate need of substantial
economic development aid. But, although the people interviewed
show drive and ambition, help does not come. It is very likely that
further population loss will come, for the needs of the people are not
being met in the mill towns.

Jim Cunningham's Comments on the Situation Today

Martha Baum conducted an interview with Jim Cunningham on
August 16, 1995. Martha and Pam devised the questions to probe

deeply into the knowledge and insights of the person who had the most extensive and intensive relationship with the River Communities Project. The setting for the interview was informal, there were no interruptions, and Jim was asked to expand as he saw fit in response to the probes. In the first question, Jim was asked specifically: Has progress been made in the mill towns to develop a unified direction for future economic development?

Jim answered that 17 communities or clusters of communities now belong to the Mon Valley Initiative programs. This means that they have plans for development but not necessarily very comprehensive ones. Different foci may be emphasized, e.g., housing, financing, business, banks. Up to now county government officials have not really been of much help in the Valley, but there are new county commissioners, and perhaps they will be able to come up with something. Michael Dawida (a new county commissioner), for example, expressed some good ideas at one time, although they did not come to anything. Some leaders feel the need for a regional coalition of community leaders to work to get resources from various sources. Some leaders feel the need for state and federal government input because local resources are meager. Tracy Soska, Director of Continuing Education in the School of Social Work, meets with them regularly to help plan strategies.

There have been, says Jim, other hopeful ideas about bringing about less isolation and more opportunities to participate in the larger city and county job possibilities. One has been the Mon Valley Expressway, a tantalizing vision that the Commonwealth of Pennsylvania says there is still insufficient money to complete. The expressway, which would link the mill towns to the new airport, is still under construction but entirely stops at Route 51, where it was supposed to be extended into the Valley. The Pennsylvania Turnpike Authority also says it has no money. After many years of promises, people may be losing faith in this option for economic improvement.

What is Jim's assessment of how people in the communities that were involved view the River Communities Project? Jim thinks most people would not even know the name or anything about the activities undertaken. Some leaders, he felt, would certainly remember and value the enterprise. Leaders involved in the Aliquippa Alliance for Unity and Development and the Mon Valley Initiative would remember the River Communities Project favorably. There was so much going on, according to Jim, that it is hard to distinguish what was valuable, but certainly these two community organization efforts were essential to survival.

Asked whether the leaders of the communities have a vision of where they want to be down the road, Jim pointed out that the Mon Valley has diversified leadership and several major forces for development with no great consensus among them. The Mon Valley Initiative represents one view on how to proceed, while both government and nongovernment development planners have other ideas. No overall agreement on development strategies and, not surprisingly, considerable rivalry and criticism are found among opposing forces.

Turning again to the River Communities Project and some of its major enterprises, Jim was asked whether the school or any faculty members were still engaged with any of the partners in the Youth Enterprise Projects. Jim answered that the Monessen group involved in the youth projects had disbanded and that no additional activity could be expected there. ELDI, long an important group in East Liberty, is in bad shape now and involved in racial disputes that may force its demise after 15 years. In Aliquippa, Cathy Cairns, as mentioned earlier, has resigned from AAUD, but Pauline Cooper has now assumed the directorship. The AAUD is still healthy and youth enterprise efforts continue. The School is still involved in various ways, but contact is now more intermittent than in the past.

THE SEQUEL
TO THE RIVER COMMUNITIES PROJECT

Even before the River Communities Project activities came to an end, a seventh seminar was added to the Seminar Series on March 21, 1987, to discuss a most urgent issue that emerged from the project findings. One of the major barriers to recovery that was identified in the action research concerned the plight of African Americans in the mill towns. The discussion in the seventh seminar focused on the worsening poverty of black people in a climate of latent racial hostility that divides and paralyzes communities. As a consequence of the evidence and the ideas and suggestions from this last seminar, a new project, the Poverty, Race, and Opportunity Project, was initiated at the School of Social Work.

The first draft of a funding proposal appeared on October 2, 1989, stating the perceived problems as follows:

> Almost a decade after the harsh economic recessions of 1980 and 1981-82, at a time when major economic indicators point to growth and recovery, there remain deep pools of joblessness and poverty in large sections of the Pittsburgh region, much of it seemingly related to discrimination against minorities and women. Existing public policies appear inadequate to cope with these localized crises. There is a need for a detailed and accurate accounting of the region's poverty and discrimination as of 1990, prepared jointly with policymakers empowered to make changes. (Poverty, Race, Opportunity, First Draft, October 2, 1989, p. 1)

On the same page, the proposal offered examples of the evidence supporting the claims that racial and gender prejudice were operating in the communities and preventing cohesive action among residents:

* Recent surveys directed by Social Work faculty in six river communities found a 19 percent poverty rate among employed black heads of households, but only an 8 percent rate for whites.
* Throughout the river communities of the region, blacks suffer substantially more difficulty finding jobs and obtaining job training. In some towns with large black populations where jobs are expanding, the new jobs tend to go to whites from outside the town. Braddock is a case in point.
* In its efforts to open and operate a small business incubator in all-white West Aliquippa, the Aliquippa Alliance for Unity and Development has faced vandalism, threats, and intimidation directed against the biracial character of its operation.
* Whereas blacks were once the single, identifiable group set apart by an extraordinary incidence of poverty, unemployment, and the need for skills training, the deprivation of single women now appears as great in the river communities.

On May 23, "A Pittsburgh Proposal for a Direct Action Program," requesting funding for the Poverty, Race, and Opportunity Project, was submitted to the Pittsburgh Foundation with a summary paragraph that read:

> Poverty and race are persistent barriers to recovery of the Pittsburgh Region. This is a proposal to demonstrate how to engage the region's large institutions in a systematic appraisal of their own policies and procedures toward removing barriers to opportunities for blacks and women heads of household.

Jim Cunningham's Update on the Poverty, Race, and Opportunity Project

Jim Cunningham was very glad to report on the Poverty, Race, and Opportunity Project, the direct action program adopted to mediate the barriers faced by African Americans and single female heads of households. The program was designed to engage key regional institutions in systematic efforts to open up opportunities for both groups. The starting places were with the Department of Public Welfare (DPW) and the University of Pittsburgh, both of which had already agreed to involvement. The five components of the project are as follows:

1. The Pitt Demonstration Project is a joint undertaking with the University's Affirmative Action Program, which is located in the President's office. It focuses on placing people in faculty and staff jobs. The Pitt Demonstration Project will have a community partner from outside the University (possibly the Urban League). Results of the effort will be the subject of a national conference to be held at the University when results are in and successful strategies can be passed on to others.
2. The University-Community Career Development Partnership (UCCDP) focuses on a DPW demonstration and works to prepare single female heads of household for jobs at the University of Pittsburgh and the University of Pittsburgh Medical Center. The project had a slow start but now has been awarded funds for another year from the City of Pittsburgh. Santos Torres, Jr., PhD, Associate Professor in the School of Social

Work, and Debra Welkley, MA, Project Coordinator, are in charge of operations. In a conversation with Debra, Martha Baum was told that, in order to make placements, the project people had to learn the University system and the University people had to get to know about the project goals. Once this was accomplished, African-American women began to be hired in significant numbers and to keep their jobs.

3. Public Housing Action Research was designed to identify the key needs and opportunities for the long-term poor. Rose Smiley, an advanced doctoral student, is now involved in this. With the help of student volunteers, she has collected 3,400 completed interviews from public housing residents. The goal is to develop a strategy, based on the experiences and suggestions of residents, for linking them with relevant institutions and helping them to leave dependency behind. A five-step model is evolving from the data.

4. The Coming-of-Age Project is an examination of the experiences of young people aged 20 to 25, divided by race and gender, in the school-to-work transition to identify the facilitators and barriers to a successful transition. Martha Baum, Anna McPhatter, Aaron Mann, and Don Miller, all faculty of the School of Social Work, have now collected and coded all data; as this book goes to press, an initial report is expected in September 1996.

5. Mill Town Households Action research is being conducted by Hide Yamatani, Professor in the School of Social Work. He is checking on the changing human condition in the Pittsburgh area, with a focus on minorities and female heads of household. From the data he collects, he tries to make determinations of relevant institutions that could alleviate problems.

As Jim pointed out, there are other things connected to the Poverty, Race, and Opportunities Project in the school. One of the most promising ones is being conducted by Jim Cunningham and Tracy Soska. They are training more black community organizers through continuing education and certification. There are jobs out there for community workers and outreach workers; ten to 15 could be placed in jobs each year.

What Does the Future Hold?

In response to the question about the future of southwestern Pennsylvania, Jim notes that the study he and Hide Yamatani carried out in 1993 and other evidence that has been pointed out do not indicate a bright future for the area, and that is one reason why he and others in the school continue to work on problems that plague not only Pittsburgh but other cities in the United States. He does remark, however, that the population drain has slowed markedly and that there is still a fairly large population of 360,000 in the Mon Valley somehow surviving, even if sometimes on a marginal level. The community organizers and planners are still actively engaged. And there is always hope!

References

Ahlbrandt, R. (1991). Mill town decline ten years later. *American Psychological Association* Spring, 193-203.

Ahlbrandt, R. D. and J. V. Cunningham (1979). *A new public policy for neighborhood preservation.* New York: Praeger Publishers.

Aldous, J. (1987). New views in the family life of the elderly and the near elderly. *Journal of Marriage and the Family* 49: 227-234.

Angell, R. C. (1936). *The family encounters the depression.* New York: Charles Scribner and Sons.

Atkinson, T., R. Liem, and J. H. Siem (1986). The social costs of unemployment: Implications for social support. *Journal of Health and Human Behavior* 27: 317-331.

Bakke, E. W. (1949). *Citizens without work.* New York: Yale University Press.

Ball, J. B. (1941). The old order changeth. . . . In *Golden Shadows, Duquesne's Golden Jubilee,* September, Duquesne, PA.

Bane, M.J. and D. T. Ellwood (1989). Slipping into and out of poverty: The dynamics of spells. *Journal of Human Resources,* 21(1): 1-23.

Bangs, R.L. and V.J. Singh (1990). *The state of Regio-Economic, Demographic, and Social Issues in Southwestern Pennsylvania.* Pittsburgh: University Center for Social and Urban Research, University of Pittsburgh.

Baum, M. (1989). *Student financial issues survey: A report from the School of Social Work.* Pittsburgh: University of Pittsburgh.

Baum, M. and M. Page (1991). Caring and multigenerational families. *The Gerontologist* 31(6): 762-769.

Baum, M., B. K. Shore, and K. Fleissner (1988). *When unemployment strikes: The responses of women in households.* River Communities Project Report. Pittsburgh: School of Social Work, University of Pittsburgh.

Baum, M., B. K. Shore, and K. Fleissner (1993). Women and economic crisis: The untold story. *Affilia* 8: 1.

Bell, T. (1976). *Out of this furnace.* Pittsburgh: University of Pittsburgh Press.

Bengston, V. L. and J. A. Kuypers (1970). Generational difference and the developmental stake. *Aging and Human Development* 2(1): 249-260.

Bensman, D. and R. Lynch (1987). *Rusted dreams: Hard times in the steel community.* New York: McGraw-Hill Book Company.

Biegel, D., J. Cunningham, and P. Martz (1986). Mon Valley people speak. In J. Cunningham and P. Martz (eds.), *Steel People*, River Communities Project Report. Pittsburgh: School of Social Work, University of Pittsburgh.

Biegel, D. E., J. Cunningham, H. Yamatani, and P. Martz (1989). Self-reliance and blue-collar unemployment in a steel town. *Social Work* 34(5): 399-406.

Binns, D. and G. Mars (1984). Family, community, and unemployment: A study of change. *American Sociological Review* 32: 662-695.

Blocher, E. (1984). Introduction. In E. Blocher, C. A. Cairns, J. V. Cunningham, and C. M. Hawkins (eds.), *Aliquippa: Struggle for survival in a Pittsburgh milltown, 1984 and before.* Pittsburgh: School of Social Work, University of Pittsburgh, and Center for Social and Urban Research, University of Pittsburgh.

Blocher, E., C. A. Cairns, J. V. Cunningham, and C. M. Hawkins (eds.) (1984). *Aliquippa: Struggle for survival in a Pittsburgh milltown, 1984 and before.* Pittsburgh: School of Social Work, University of Pittsburgh, and Center for Social and Urban Research, University of Pittsburgh.

Blotzer, J. (1986). Leaving the most liveable city: Graduates in Mon, Ohio valleys plan to go elsewhere for jobs. *Pittsburgh Post-Gazette,* June 18.

Bond, J. B., Jr. and C. D. Harvey (1988). *Intergenerational perceptions of family interactions.* Paper presented at the 17th Annual Meeting of the Canadian Association for Gerontology, Halifax, Nova Scotia.

Brenner, M. H. (1973). *Mental illness and the economy.* Cambridge, MA: Harvard University Press.

Brenner, M. H. (1976). *Estimating the social costs of national economic policy: Implications for mental health, physical health, and criminal aggression.* Testimony before the Joint Economic Committee, 94th Congress. Washington, DC: Government Printing Office.

Brenner, M. H. (1979). Influence of the social environment on psychopathology: The historic perspective. In J. E. Barrett (ed.), *Stress and mental disorder.* New York: Raven Press.

Brody, E. M. (1981). Women in the middle and family help to older people. *The Gerontologist* 21(5): 471-480.

Brubaker, T. H. (1985). *Later life families.* Beverley Hills, CA: Sage Publications.

Cairns, C. A. (1991). Comprehensive community effort, the Aliquippa model for remaking a battered community. Unpublished manuscript.

Cairns, C. A. (1986). The Aliquippa Alliance for Unity and Development: An organizer's perspective of the initial effort. In C. A. Cairns and J. V. Cunningham (eds.), *Aliquippa update: A Pittsburgh milltown struggles to come back,* River Communities Project Report. Pittsburgh: School of Social Work, University of Pittsburgh.

Cairns, C. A. and J. Cunningham (eds.) (1986). *Aliquippa update: A Pittsburgh milltown struggles to come back, 1984-86.* River Communities Project Report. Pittsburgh: School of Social Work, University of ittsburgh.

Cavan, R. and K. Ranck (1938). *The family and the depression.* Chicago: University of Chicago Press.

Chang, R. and A. Deinard (1982). Single father caretakers: Demographic characteristics and adjustment processes. *American Journal of Orthopsychiatry* 52(2): 236-243.

Cicerelli, V. G. (1981). *Helping elderly parents: The role of adult children.* Boston: Auburn House.

Cobb, S. (1976). Social support as a moderator of life stress. *Psychosomatic Medicine* 38(5): 300-314.

Cobb, S. and S. V. Kasl (1977). Terminations: The consequences of job loss. Washington, DC: National Institute for Occupational Safety and Health, Report No. 76-1261.

Coontz, P. D., J. Martin, and E. W. Sites (1988). *Steeltown fathers:*

Rearing children in an era of industrial decline. River Communities Project Report. Pittsburgh: School of Social Work, University of Pittsburgh.

Corcoran, K. and J. Fischer (1987). *Measures for clinical practice: A sourcebook.* New York: Free Press.

Corn, D. (1986). The Mon Valley mourns for steel. *Harper's Magazine,* September.

Coverman, S. and J. Shelley (1986). Change in men's housework and child care time. *Journal of Marriage and the Family* 48: 413-422.

Cowgill, D. O. and L. D. Holmes (eds.) (1972). *Aging and modernization.* New York: Appleton Century Crofts.

Cunningham, J. V. (1984). Borough government. In E. Blocher, C. A. Cairns, J. V. Cunningham, and C. M. Hawkins (eds.), *Aliquippa: Struggle for survival in a Pittsburgh milltown, 1984 and before.* Pittsburgh: School of Social Work, University of Pittsburgh, and Center for Social and Urban Research, University of Pittsburgh.

Cunningham, J. V. and P. Martz (eds.) (1986). *Steel People.* River Communities Project Report. Pittsburgh: School of Social Work, University of Pittsburgh.

Cunningham, J. V. and P. Martz (eds.) (1986). *Trouble in Electric Valley: Local leaders assess the difficult future of East Pittsburgh and Turtle Creek.* Pittsburgh: School of Social Work, University of Pittsburgh.

Dean, A. and N. Lin (1977). The stress-buffering role of social support. *Journal of Nervous and Mental Diseases,* pp. 403-417.

Department of Labor and Industry, Office of Employment Security (1983) *Pennsylvania Unemployment Fact Sheet,* October.

Dohrenwend, B. and B. Dohrenwend (1974). *Stressful life events: Their nature and effects.* New York: John Wiley and Sons.

Elder, G. H., Jr., R. D. Conger, E. M. Foster, and M. Ardelt (1992). Families under economic pressure. *Journal of Family Issues* 13(1): 5-37.

Erikson, E. (1994). *Identity and the life cycle.* New York: W. W. Norton & Co., Inc.

Faughnan, P., J. V. Cunningham, C. Ward, H. Burke, D. Feehan, B. Kenney, C. Cairns, D. O'Brien, D. Candy, and E. Murphy (1987).

Threatened Generation, a proposal for an international demonstration. Collaborative publication: University College, Dublin, Ireland, and the School of Social Work, University of Pittsburgh.

Ferree, M. (1984). Sacrifice, satisfaction, and social change: Women's employment and the family. In K. Sacks and D. Remy (eds.), *My troubles are going to have trouble with me.* New Brunswick, NJ: Rutgers University Press.

Fessler, D. R. (1976). *Facilitating community change: A basic guide.* La Jolla, CA: University Associates.

Figley, C. R. and H. I. McCubbin (1983). *Stress and the Family,* vol. 2. New York: Brunner/Mazel.

Gore, S. (1978). The effects of social support in moderating the health consequences of unemployment. *Journal of Health and Social Behavior* 19: 157-165.

Hagestad, G. O. (1984). Women in intergenerational patterns of power and influence. (pp. 37-55). In L. Stamm and C. D. Ryff (eds.) *Social Power and the influence of women.* Boulder, CO: Westview Press.

Hagestad, G. O. (1985). Older women in intergenerational relationships. (pp. 137-151). In M. R. Haug, A. B. Ford, and M. Sheafor (eds.) *The physical and mental health of aged women.* Boulder, CO: Westview Press.

Hawkins, C. M. (1984). Economic problems and human impacts. In E. Blocher, C. A. Cairns, J. V. Cunningham, and C. M. Hawkins (eds.), *Aliquippa: Struggle for survival in a Pittsburgh milltown, 1984 and before.* Pittsburgh: School of Social Work, University of Pittsburgh, and Center for Social and Urban Research, University of Pittsburgh.

Hawkins, M. (1986). Homestead Community Credit Union: Comeback mechanism for a depressed river town. In J. Cunningham and P. Martz (eds.), *Steel People*, River Communities Project Report. Pittsburgh: School of Social Work, University of Pennsylvania.

Hochschild, A. and A. Machung (1990). *The second shift.* New York: Avon.

Hoerr, J. P. (1988). *And the wolf finally came.* Pittsburgh: University of Pittsburgh Press.

Horowitz, A. (1985). Sons and daughters as caregivers to older parents: Differences in role performance and consequences. *The Gerontologist* 25(6): 612-617.

Hudson, W. W. (1982). The clinical instrument package: A field manual. Chicago: Dorsey Press.

Humphrey, C. R., and R. S. Krannick (1980). The promotion of growth in small urban places and its impact on population change, 1975-78. *Social Science Quarterly* 61 (December): 581-594.

Jahoda, M. (1979) The impact of unemployment in the 1930s and the 1970s. *Bulletin of the British Psychological Society* 30.

Kahn, R. L. and T. C. Antonucci (1983). Social supports of the elderly: Family/friends/professionals. Final report to the National Institute of Aging.

Kohn, M. (1989). *Class and conformity: A study in values.* Homewood, IL: Dorsey Press.

Komarovsky, M. (1987). *Blue collar marriage.* New York: Random House.

Kranichfeld, M. L. (1987). Rethinking family power. *Journal of Family Issues* 8(1): 42-56.

Lamb, M. (1982). *The role of the father in child development.* New York: Wiley & Sons.

LaRossa, R. and M. LaRossa (1981). *Transition to parenthood: How infants change families.* Beverley Hills, CA: Sage Publications.

Larson, J. H. (1984). The effect of husband's unemployment on marital and family relations. *Family Relations,* 33, pp. 503-511.

Liem R. and J. Liem (1979). Social support and stress: Some general issues and their application to unemployment. In *Mental health and the economy*, L. Ferman and J. Gordus (eds.) Kalamazoo, Michigan: W.E. Upjohn Institute.

Liem R. and P. Rayman (1982). Health and social costs of unemployment: Research and policy consideration. *American Psychologist* 37(10): 1116-1123.

Lowy, L. (1988). *Social work with the aging,* 2d ed. New York: Longman, Inc.

Margolis, M., R. E. Burtt, and J. McLaughlin (1986). Impact of Industrial Decline: Braddock, North Braddock, and Rankin. In J. Cunningham and P. Martz (eds.), *Steel People*. River Communities Project Report. Pittsburgh: School of Social Work, University of Pittsburgh.

Martinez-Brawley, E. E. (1990). *Perspectives on the small community.* Silver Spring, MD: National Association of Social Workers Press.

McCubbin, H. I. and J. M. Patterson (1983). The family stress process: The double ABCX model of adjustment and adaptation. *Marriage and Family Review* 6: 7-87.

McLloyd, V. C. (1989). Socialization and development in a changing society: The effects of parental job and income loss on children. *American Psychologist* 44: 293-302.

Miller, S. K. (1986). Local borough governments. In J. Cunningham and P. Martz (eds.), *Trouble in Electric Valley: Local leaders assess the difficult future of East Pittsburgh and Turtle Creek.* Pittsburgh: School of Social Work, University of Pittsburgh.

Modany, D., and J. V. Cunningham (1986). Business outlook. In C. A. Cairns and J. V. Cunningham (eds.), *Aliquippa Update: A Pittsburgh milltown struggles to come back, 1984-86.* River Communities Project Report. Pittsburgh: School of Social Work, University of Pittsburgh.

Moen, P. (1983). Unemployment, public policy, and families: Forecast for the 1980s. *Journal of Marriage and the Family* 45(5): 751-758.

Murray, C. (1984). *Losing ground.* New York: Basic Books.

Nash, N. C. (1987). Data that Appear Good, Some Detect New Poverty. *The New York Times*, August 8, A9.

Newman, K. S. (1988). *Falling from grace.* New York: Random.

Page, M. H. and M. Silverman (1987). *The impact of unemployment: The elderly and their families.* River Communities Project Report. Pittsburgh: School of Social Work, University of Pittsburgh.

Perlmutter, E. M. (1988). Aid aims to halt exodus of youths. *Pittsburgh Press,* November 21, 1988.

Powell, D. H. and P. F. Driscoll (1973). Middle-class professionals face unemployment. *Society,* January-February, 18-26.

Radloff, L. (1977). The CES-D scale: A self report depression scale for research in the general population. *Applied Psychological Measurement* 1(3): 385-401.

Rankin, J. (1990). An economic shield for PA families? *McKeesport (Pa.) Daily News,* November 20.

Rischell, G. (1989). Irish connection: Pitt, Dublin school cooperating in youth enterprise program. *Pittsburgh Post-Gazette,* February 11, 1989.

River Communities Project. (1989) Evaluation of the Unemployed Council of Southwestern Pennsylvania. Pittsburgh: River Communities Project, School of Social Work, University of Pittsburgh.

Robb, C. (1984). Social control organizations. In E. Blocher, C. A. Cairns, J. V. Cunningham, and C. M. Hawkins (eds.), *Aliquippa: Struggle for survival in a Pittsburgh milltown, 1984 and before.* Pittsburgh: School of Social Work, University of Pittsburgh, and Center for Social and Urban Research, University of Pittsburgh.

Robinson, J. (1988). Who's doing the housework? *American Demographics* 63: 24-28.

Rosenthal, C. J. (1985). Kinkeeping in the family division of labor. *Journal of Marriage and the Family* 7: 965-974.

Rubin, A. and E. Babbie (1992). *Research methods for social work,* 2d ed. Belmont, CA: Wadsworth, Inc.

Rusman, A. (1990). *The Monessen story: A school district joins its community's economic recovery effort.* River Communities Project Report. Pittsburgh: University of Pittsburgh, School of Social Work.

Scholzman, K.L. (1979). Women and Unemployment: Assessing the biggest myths in women–A feminist perspective (2d ed.) J. Freeman. (ed.) Palo Alto, CA: Mayfield Publishers.

Seaberry, J. (1986). White Men Losers in Wage Race. *The Washington Post,* December 10, A6.

Sidel, R. (1986). *Women and children last: The plight of poor women in America.* New York: Penguin Books.

Singh, V. P. and R. L. Bangs (1990). The State of the region–economic, demographic, and social issues in Southwestern Pennsylvania. Pittsburgh, PA: University Center for Social and Urban Research, University of Pittsburgh.

Smeeding, T. (1990). Economic status of the elderly. *Handbook of aging and the social sciences,* 3d ed. San Diego: Academic Press.

Smith, R. E. (1979). The movement of women into the labor force.

In R. E. Smith (ed.), *The subtle revolution: Women and work.* Washington, DC: The Urban Institute.

Sussman, M. B. (1986). The family life of old people. In R. Binstock and E. Shanas (eds.), *Handbook of aging and the social sciences,* 2d ed. New York: Van Nostrand Reinhold.

Thompson, D. B. (1985). The human trauma of steel's decline. *Industry Week,* September 2, 43.

Unger, D. and D. H. Powell (1980). Supporting families under stress: The role of social networks. *Family Relations* October, 566-574.

United States Department of Health and Human Services (1987). *Married and unmarried couples.* Washington, DC: The National Center for Health Services.

U.S. Congress, Joint Economic Committee of Congress, Office of Technology Assessment (1986). "Plant Closing: Advance Notice & Rapid Response." Special Report, Washington, DC: Government Printing Office.

U.S. Congress, Office of Technology Assessment (1986). *Technology and structural unemployment:*

Reemploying displaced adults: Summary, OTA-ITE-251. Washington, DC: U.S. Government Printing Office.

Voydanoff, P. (1983). Unemployment: Family strategies of adaptation. In C. R. Figley and H. I. McCubbin (eds.), *Stress and the family,* vol. 2. New York: Brunner/Mazel.

Voydanoff, P. and B. W. Donnelly (1988). Economic distress, family coping, and the quality of family life. In P. Voydanoff and L. C. Majka (eds.), *Families and economic distress: Coping strategies and social policy.* Beverly Hills, CA: Sage Publications.

Voydanoff, P. and Majka, L. C. (eds.) (1988). *Families and economic distress: Coping strategies and social policy.* Beverly Hills, CA: Sage Publications.

Wagner, D. (1991). Reviving the action research model: Combining case and cause with dislocated workers. *Social Work* 36(6): 477-482.

Waltz, T. and V. Groze (1991). The mission of social work revisited. *Social Work* 36(6): 50-55.

Webb, N. (1984). *Preschool children with working parents.* New York: University Press of America.

Weitzman, L. J. (1981). *The marriage contract: Spouses, lovers, and the law.* New York: Free Press.

Yamatani, H. and J. V. Cunningham (1993). *The Mon Valley workforce survey, 1993.* Pittsburgh: School of Social Work and University Center for Social and Urban Research, University of Pittsburgh.

Yamatani, H., L. Maguire, M. L. O'Kennedy, and R. Rogers (1988). *Battered households.* River Communities Project Report. Pittsburgh: School of Social Work, University Pennsylvania.

Yamatani, H., L. Maguire, R. Rogers, and M. O'Kennedy (1989). *The impact of social/economic change on households among six communities in western Pennsylvania.* Pittsburgh: University of Pittsburgh.

Zastrow, Charles (1985). *The practice of social work,* 2d ed. Homewood, IL: Dorsey Press.

Zimmerman, S. L. (1988). *Understanding family policy: Theoretical approaches.* Beverly Hills, CA: Sage Publications.

Index